77 Ways

TO PERFECT YOUR
COMMUNICATIONS SKILLS

ALSO BY FRANK H. LEONE

Marketing Healthcare Services to Employers:
Strategies and Tactics
2012

Occupational Health Sales
and Marketing for a New Era
2010

77 Ways

TO PERFECT YOUR COMMUNICATIONS SKILLS

*Enhancing Your Personal
and Professional Relationships*

by Frank H. Leone

FOREWORD BY MITCH GODDARD

THE 77
GROUP

2020

DEDICATION

Nothing means more in life than family.

To my wonderful parents, Dorothy and Frank Sr.; in-laws, Terry and Ray Mainini; Diane—my wife of more than 40 years; our son, Ryan; his partner, Karina, our grandson, Nikko; my brothers-in-law, Ron and Steve; my sister-in-law, Sharon; our nephews, Kevin and Michael; our nieces, Melissa, Gianna, Elisa, and Mandie; and our beloved lab, Brava.

"The single biggest problem in communication is the illusion that it has taken place."

*— attributed to playwright
George Bernard Shaw*

CONTENTS

PART III.

WRITTEN COMMUNICATION

PART IV.

SMALL-GROUP PRESENTATIONS

PART V.

PUBLIC SPEAKING—PREPARATION

PART VI.

PUBLIC SPEAKING—PRESENTATION

PART VII.
NONVERBAL COMMUNICATION

PART VIII.
EMAIL COMMUNICATION

PART IX.
OTHER FORMS OF COMMUNICATION

FOREWORD

MY FIRST MEMORY of Frank Leone takes me back to 2007 when he opened a seminar that I attended.

I was quickly drawn to Frank's easygoing, genuine, and affable style. He was quick-witted, humorous, and informative and brought a healthy dose of fun to what I thought was going to be an agonizing two and a half days of learning. An accomplished storyteller, Frank shared tales about himself along with real-life business encounters that were attention grabbing and relatable. Each account was germane to the subject matter and usually wrapped with a valuable tip for success.

During the seminar, he shared that he lived in Santa Barbara, where he ran RYAN Associates, the company he founded in 1985. Having lived in Santa Barbara myself, I found an excuse to strike up a conversation with him during a lunch break. Chatting him up, I was able to confirm that my first impression of Frank was on target. He was smart, approachable, and fun, and we shared similar interests, among them, the same favorite Santa Barbara restaurant. Our first encounter ended in an agreement to meet there for a meal and a glass of wine. I was skeptical that it would ever happen, but it did—on several occasions—and our friendship was born.

The next year I became a regular attendee at RYAN Associates' annual conference. I got to know Frank's team, networked with others in the industry, and grew my knowledge base. I looked forward to these annual events because they were fun, and I always came away with something of value, be it useful new intel or a fresh business contact.

Frank charismatically captured and held everyone's attention during these conferences. He gave general-assembly talks, moderated panel discussions, and taught a few courses himself, while maintaining high visibility as he moved through a well-coordinated conference schedule and its associated social activities. He was well known, liked, and respected, and I observed others maneuvering for precious one-on-one time with him. As people approached him, I marveled at his gracious transition from person to person while staying on task as host and conference coordinator.

Fast forward to January 2019. I received a Happy Birthday text message from Frank. Surprised that he even knew my birthday, I responded, and, in short order, we were making plans to meet for dinner. Arriving a few minutes late, I was greeted with his usual big hug, and we talked about how our professional interests might align. We shared our ideas and agreed to continue to explore the possibility of collaborating on a project. I left that night with a good feeling for time well spent, along with golden nuggets of wisdom and plenty to think about.

About six months later we arrived at a decision crossroad. Did our values, intentions, and visions align? If so, were we ready to commit to a partnership?

We agreed to move forward with shared confidence and trust. Within 90 days, we had developed and launched a strategic plan, determined methods and platforms to best execute our vision, identified supporting contractors, chosen a name for our enterprise and, oh yeah, Frank completed this manuscript! For a man looking to "slow down," Frank continues to be vibrant, creative, and dedicated to making a difference by serving others.

As you read this book, I am confident you will agree that Frank is a subject-matter expert. He is among the few professionals qualified to share his experience, insights, and expertise on the concepts necessary to become an effective communicator. As a bonus, he has packaged it in a fun, easy, and relatable read with simple steps to implement his suggestions and ideas.

Enjoy!

MITCH GODDARD
March 2020

PREFACE

At approximately 4 p.m. on April 12, 2017, I boarded the Pacific Surfliner at the San Diego Amtrak station, bound for my hometown of Santa Barbara. An hour earlier I had presented a final consulting report to senior management at the UC San Diego (UCSD) Medical Center and, in doing so, wrapped up my working career. After 31 years, 7 months, and 798 client engagements, I was ending my involvement with the company I had founded in 1985 and sold in 2016. After more than half a century in the workforce, I was suddenly on an endless summer vacation.

I had no big retirement plan. I felt comfortable letting life and events unfold for a while, remaining open to opportunities and ideas as they arose. *Que será será*. I had a vague notion that I might soon put my public-speaking experience to use, talking about issues such as prison reform, the horror of drug addiction, and firearms laws, among others. But that spark never happened.

I spent the next two and a half years working out daily, playing golf, closely following the sordid politics of our day, rooting for my beloved Mets, staying in touch with scores of friends, enjoying time with my wife of 40 years; my only child, Ryan; and our new grandson. Life was good. But something was missing.

Enter Mitch Goddard. I met Mitch around 2007 when he was a student at one of my sales training courses. His health system later became an important consulting client, and we became friends—and an odd couple in many respects. Mitch has a varied background spanning four decades excelling in leadership roles across multiple industries. During his time with the Department of Defense, he honed many of the skills that largely define his style (focusing on "Honor, Courage, and Commitment") while leading high-performing teams and facilitating leadership training in coordination with the National War College.

Mitch resides in Hanford, California, about four hours north of Santa Barbara, and had recently established the Goddard Leadership Institute. The concept of leadership fascinated me enough that I flirted with the idea of returning to my undergraduate alma mater, Vanderbilt, to pursue a doctorate in education with an emphasis in leadership. It turned out that neither Vanderbilt nor I thought it made sense to confer such a pragmatic degree on someone who would be approaching their 80th birthday upon completion of the degree.

Out of the embers of this flirtation, however, came a plan: Mitch and I would pool our talents to form The 77 Group. We decided to launch this collaboration by publishing two books: the first written by me about communication and the second written by Mitch on leadership. We agreed that each book would reflect 77 different concepts, a number chosen because we both met our wives in 1977, only five days apart, that spring.

My favorite quote is from Shakespeare's *Hamlet,* the advice spoken by Polonius:

> *This above all: to thine own self be true,*
> *And it must follow, as the night the day,*
> *Thou canst not then be false to any man.*

I have tried to write this book in the spirit of that quote, ensuring that my writing style reflects my personality, that it is easy to read, with concise short points rather than wordy philosophy, is filled with personal anecdotes and a healthy dose of attempted, often self-effacing, humor. In short, I wanted to write a book on communication that would be quick, to the point, engaging, and fun.

I feel that my life experience, both on and off the professional playing field, has taught me many lessons about communication. I want to share these lessons with others through the distribution of this book before they are lost to history.

As I state in the pages that follow, the written word is forever. Who can deny that someone, somewhere, may read a tattered copy of this book or be privy to an electronic version of it in some corner of cyberspace in 2120 or later and, as a result, enhance their life in some manner?

As my long-ago professional mentor, Dr. Barry Levy, often stated, "One person can make a difference." If this book can help even one person, it will be well worth my investment in time and toil.

FRANK H. LEONE
Santa Barbara, California
April 2020

Please enjoy this book and let me know your thoughts (frankhleone@gmail.com or frank@77grp.com).

77 Ways

TO PERFECT YOUR
COMMUNICATIONS SKILLS

I

INTRODUCTION

Half the world is composed of people who have something to say and can't, and the other half who have nothing to say and keep on saying it.

—poet Robert Frost

1

COMMIT TO BECOMING A GREAT COMMUNICATOR

MY JOURNEY AS an effective communicator began inauspiciously. A fifth-grade classmate stuttered terribly. Apparently, my empathy for him was so great that I soon acquired a similar stammer. It lasted through most of high school and transformed me from a fun-loving extrovert to a quiet teenage dreamer, aka "El Silencio." At that time, the thought of becoming a public speaker, let alone a busy, respected one, was as far-fetched as walking on Mars.

Fast forward to 1982. I had just moved from California to Massachusetts and was at a pivotal point in the early stage of my career when I began to notice that many extremely successful people in both business and politics had little on the ball other than being strong public speakers. Eureka! The stairway to success! I vowed then and there to become the strongest communicator I could possibly be. I made myself a student of the most compelling speakers in the nation, sitting in the front row of every presentation in order to soak up everything I could about their oratorical techniques.

At the time, I was executive director of a hospital-based aeromedical program—a helicopter service—that provided limitless opportunities for me to speak before groups such as first responders, hospital personnel, and myriad other health-related professional associations. Surprise! As the frequency of my engagements increased, so did my confidence. Each event reinforced the axiom that effective communicators are made, not born.

And it all began with a firm commitment to become a better communicator.

MINI STEPS TO SUCCESS

1. Be honest with yourself. Determine if you *really* want to devote the time required to evolve into a polished communicator. For example, you can just thumb through this book and most likely enhance your communication performance to some degree. But if you want to become a "great" communicator, I suggest you dive into the book full throttle.

2. Put your commitment in context. Why are you doing this? What result do you wish to achieve? What are the steps you need to take to reach your desired level of proficiency?

3. Identify exceptional communicators in your community and monitor them closely. For example, politicians, despite their many failings, are often strong communicators (even if their message is nonsense). Get a front-row seat at their speeches. Listen to every word and watch every gesture. Adapt, as appropriate, what you learn.

4. Monitor your own performance, whether it's

during a one-on-one conversation, in a real-time presentation, or in a written text. After every instance, ask yourself if the way you communicated met or exceeded your expectations. If the answer is no, identify how you fell short.

———THE TAKEAWAY———

Becoming a great communicator requires planning, discipline, and effort. Your time is precious, but so are the extraordinary personal and professional benefits that great communicators inevitably reap.

To dream the impossible dream
To fight the unbeatable foe
To bear with unbearable sorrow
To run where the brave dare not go
—lyricist Joe Darion,
"To Dream the Impossible Dream"

2

BE REALISTIC AND MAINTAIN PERSPECTIVE

THERE IS NOTHING inherently wrong with dreaming the impossible dream. Indeed, many of the world's greatest artistic, scientific, and other professional breakthroughs have been built on the back of seemingly pie-in-the-sky hopes.

Yet more dreams than not are unrealistic from the start and never come near to achieving their objective. Caution and perspective are advised.

Once you have committed to becoming a better communicator (and who wouldn't want to become a better communicator?) and have a plan in place, take a close look at its viability. Ask yourself if your communication development plan is consistent with your long-term objectives. Is it realistic for you, given your present skills? Is it too ambitious for your schedule? Or, conversely, is it unnecessarily modest?

In short, it's reality check time.

MINI STEPS TO SUCCESS

1. Soberly assess your communication assets and deficits. What are your strengths? What needs improvement? And what may or may not be possible? Recording your findings in a notebook or journal will sharpen your focus and provide an ongoing assessment.

2. Ask close friends, professional colleagues, and family what they think are your greatest communication assets and in what areas they believe you can improve. Reality is usually better defined by measuring your perceptions against the perspectives of those who know you best.

3. List your communications objectives and match each one with a communication asset that you bring to the table.

4. Similarly, list your deficits and determine, in writing, what you need to do to overcome each of them.

5. Schedule a self-awareness reality check once a month. Do it on your own, with a colleague or staff member, or both. Ask yourself what is working and why. Then consider what is not working (and may be unlikely to ever work). Beware of the unachievable. In most instances, it's best to walk away from something that is likely to nag at you indefinitely.

THE TAKEAWAY

Establish a series of goals and then measure the likelihood of achieving each of them against your inherent capabilities, your situation, and where each goal fits within current and forecastable communication trends.

By failing to prepare, you are preparing to fail.
—founding father Benjamin Franklin

3

DEVELOP A PROACTIVE COMMUNICATIONS PLAN

AS I TYPE THESE WORDS in my home office, I am reminded that our house is the realization of a blueprint that someone designed 95 years ago. Virtually all successful organizations or products started with a well-conceived and executed plan. It stands to reason that a detailed plan should also be developed if you want to raise your communication skills to a higher level.

I do not recommend a specific must-do format for a personal communications plan. A plan, however, should be completed in writing and be as brief and readable as possible (1-2 pages).

> *THE CORE STRUCTURE SHOULD RESEMBLE A CLASSIC MARKETING PLAN:*

- *Objective: What are your short and long-term objectives? Why do you want to be a better communicator, and, ultimately, where do you want to be both professionally and personally in [fill-in-the-blank] years?*

- *Internal-external assessment:What are your inherent communication strengths and what are your primary communications challenges (your internal assessment)? This was covered in Chapter 1. However, it bears repeating here, because strengths and weaknesses should be incorporated into your plan. What specific communication skills do you need in order to make the greatest impact in your professional and personal worlds (your external assessment)?*

- *Strategy and tactics: What strategies will you employ to become a stronger communicator? For example, these might include reading relevant books, learning from strong speakers, or practicing before both live and imaginary audiences. What specific tasks do you need to complete to implement your strategies?*

- *Action calendar: Put your steps in chronological order. Plans can be broken into a variety of time intervals, such as weekly, monthly, or quarterly. I suggest breaking your plan down by months. This is not too broad, yet it's broad enough to give your schedule a little wiggle room. Don't forget that an action calendar is only as effective as your commitment to following it.*

MINI STEPS TO SUCCESS

1. Commit to writing a short, concise personal communications development plan.

2. Document where you are, where you want to be, what you are going to do in order to get there, and when each step should take place.

3. Refer to your plan continuously, amend it as necessary, and try to stay on schedule.

4. Do not rest on your laurels. Update your plan annually.

Your visions will become clear only when
you can look into your own heart.
Who looks outside, dreams; who looks inside, awakes.

—psychiatrist Carl Jung

4

KNOW THYSELF: EMBRACE INTERNAL COMMUNICATION MESSAGES

COMMUNICATION GOES BEYOND communicating with others; it is also about communicating with yourself. Talk to yourself. (Warning: not while you're walking alone down Main Street.) Ask yourself who you really are and who you want to be. Be generous and fair to yourself by noting how, when, and with whom you communicate well and, conversely, how, when, and with whom you communicate poorly.

Internal communication is all about self-reflection and total honesty. If you delude yourself into thinking your communication skills are stronger or weaker than they really are, everything you learn in this book will be compromised.

Your strongest assets will become the building blocks for better communication skills in the future. A sober assessment that addresses the features of your communication liabilities should be the focus of your communication plan.

Strike a careful—and accurate—balance between self-confidence and humility.

MINI STEPS TO SUCCESS

1. Review your communication strengths and weaknesses.

2. Create two lists: those with whom you interact personally and professional contacts. The first list will likely include spouses, offspring, friends, and neighbors. The second might range from senior management to support personnel.

3. Consider all the ways you communicate, including in-person one-on one conversations, telephone calls, group meetings, speeches before large groups, email communications, and text messages. Assess how well you perform in each of these situations.

4. Initially concentrate on your communications strengths. In which settings and kinds of messages do you excel? Identify as best as you can why some types of communication support your strengths more than others.

5. Inventory your most pronounced communication weaknesses. Why do you think you fall short?

6. Keep an ongoing list. Every time you communicate well or poorly, jot down your finding and add it to a master document.

Avoid self-delusion. Reflect on who you really are. Where do you really want to be, and what will it take for you to get there? Be 100 percent honest. No one else needs to know.

*Memory is the treasure house of the mind wherein
the monuments thereof are kept and preserved.*
—17th-century historian Thomas Fuller

5

TAKE NOTES: NEVER LET A GREAT IDEA OR IMPORTANT FACT GO UNDOCUMENTED

CONFESSION: As I get older (and older and older and older) there are more things that I am certain I will remember that I quickly forget. The moral of the story? Do not rely strictly on your memory if you can cover your bases by taking notes.

A strong communicator should have a sturdy grasp of relevant facts. Too many facts come our way during any given day for even the most alert of us to remember them all. And passing on incorrect information can easily negate the positive effects of your communications.

Note taking goes beyond scrupulously recording facts. New ideas—both great or just fair ones—often are marked only with a shrug of our shoulders and a message to self: "I need to remember that." Accordingly, you should devise a system whereby new ideas can be recorded as you hear or think of them. Granted, many will not retain the same appeal as they had when you first recorded them, but if even a few survive the light of day you are ahead of the game.

MINI STEPS TO SUCCESS

1. Find a way to record critical information or ideas. It might be as simple as using the notes section of a smartphone, keeping a small notepad in your pocket or purse, or carrying a tablet or laptop.

2. If possible, dictate your information rather than typing or writing it in. Dictation takes less time and makes it easier to record fleeting thoughts.

3. Assign new information to appropriate computer files. Perhaps the information is an idea you wish to include in a future speech or group presentation. Perhaps it's data that can be applied to an argument in support of a position. In other words, anticipate how you will use this new information or idea and put it somewhere that is logical and thus easily retrieved.

4. Regardless of the nature of your new information or idea, be prepared to record the source of the information. That might mean "as reported in last week's *New York Times*" or "overheard in the locker room of the gym." Credibility is important.

———THE TAKEAWAY———

Make a habit of documenting every insight, piece of information, and idea you come up with or encounter in real time. Dictating new ideas and action steps in the notes section of your mobile device is a fast and easy way to do this. Do not let a relevant fact or promising idea fade away.

I can't deny the fact that you like me,
right now, you like me!
—actress Sally Field's 1984
Oscar acceptance speech

6

BE LIKEABLE, HUMBLE, AND FRIENDLY AND SHOW RESPECT

W HAT WAS AT THE time a new and notable lesson was learned as a result of polling following the first 1960 presidential debate between Richard M. Nixon and John F. Kennedy. Polls after the debate indicated that a majority of those who only heard the event on radio felt Nixon had won the debate, whereas a majority of those who saw it on television thought Kennedy was the victor. Words assuredly do matter, but so do the visual cues one gives when delivering those words.

Whether you are speaking one-on-one or in front of a group, personal likability will affect how well your message is received. Of course, at the end of the day, we are who we are, and not everyone is going to cotton to our unique personality. And yet the connections we forge with people can be proactively modified by focusing on how we present ourselves, not merely by what we say.

For example, people tend to be more likeable if they smile frequently, appear humble, or even seem self-effacing. It helps if they are visibly at ease and can connect with their audience by being one of them.

Showing respect to your audience, whether that's an

individual, a group of individuals, or the recipient of an email message, is also essential. Whenever possible, offer sincere praise to groups as well as individuals, and be certain to thank people for their invaluable, and always finite, time.

MINI STEPS TO SUCCESS

1. Begin with humility. No one likes a pompous know-it-all. However, we often have a defense mechanism that causes us to cover up our usual humility. Being humble won't make you appear weak; embrace humility.

2. As the old shampoo ad reminds us, "You only have one chance to make a good first impression." Begin every communication with a statement exuding sincerity and gratitude. ("I recognize how valuable your time is" or "I appreciate your finding a few minutes for me.") One should never get tired of thanking their audience.

3. Be yourself. People easily detect false airs. If you are funny, go for it. If you are a natural storyteller, go for that, too. If you are not, don't force it. If you are a card-carrying member of the humorless class, don't even try.

4. Share your fallibility. ("When I was younger, I mistakenly thought....")

5. Learn to read your audience (both in one-on-one interactions and when addressing a group). Recognize when you are connecting with them and

when you are not. Early in my speaking career, I learned how to read the facial expressions and body language of my audience and how to instantly adapt to what I saw, either by juicing up or simmering down my communication style.

————THE TAKEAWAY————

Identify your likeable qualities and become comfortable in your own skin. When you do, you will make others feel comfortable as well. And always show respect to your audience. They are giving you their time and attention.

Walk a mile in my shoes, walk a mile in my shoes,
Hey, before you abuse, criticize and accuse,
Walk a mile in my shoes.
—-singer-songwriter Joe South,
"Walk a Mile in My Shoes"

7

WALK A MILE IN SOMEONE'S SHOES

AS IMPORTANT AS your verbal and written words may be, the filter through which your communication is received will be equally, if not more, important than what you say. In other words, how your words are interpreted is more relevant to your message than its actual content.

Given the importance of your audience's point of view, it makes sense to evaluate your crowd as best you can before constructing your message. If you are communicating to an individual, think about what is most important to them. What are their hot buttons; what are their ultimate needs? What is that person's personality style? That is, are they dominant or submissive? Cautious or reckless? High or low energy? And how will that style affect their perceptions?

If you are communicating with a group, what is that group's perspective? What are their inherent interests and what are likely to be their collective blind spots? What are the key words, phrases, or concepts that will resonate with them?

An excellent way to get into the other person's shoes is to simply ask them straightforward and potentially revealing questions. What is important to them? What would be their optimal outcome? What are their greatest fears and concerns? Minimize simple yes-or-no questions and probe with in-depth, open-ended questions. Be careful not to assume too much. Hidden biases often lurk just beneath the surface.

MINI STEPS TO SUCCESS

1. Before you initiate a conversation, speak to a small group, or make a public presentation, ask yourself how the views and needs of your audience might be similar or different from your position.

2. Identify words, phrases, and concepts that will resonate with the intended recipients of your message.

3. Gather insight in real time by asking questions. When you are speaking one-on-one, seek the other party's opinion. If you are speaking to a large group, throw out some questions at the outset and ask for a show of hands. The earlier and better you know your audience the more likely you are to successfully tailor your communication to best get through to them.

4. To a degree that is comfortable for you, reflect the other party's personality. If they are jovial, be jovial. If they are concerned or angry, be empathetic and serious. If they are technical, be technical. If they are big-picture oriented, express your thoughts from a big-picture perspective.

——THE TAKEAWAY——

Before you utter or write a word, put yourself in the other party's shoes: Who are they? What is important to them? How will they filter your words? At the end of the day, effective communication is about connecting with others.

Tell me why you cried, and why you lied to me
Tell me why you cried, and why you lied to me
—Beatles John Lennon and Paul McCartney,
"Tell Me Why"

8

PREDETERMINE AND STATE YOUR OBJECTIVES

I T IS HARD FOR any of us to make it through an entire day without someone writing or saying something to us that is lacking context. In daily one-on-one conversations, I often have the thought, "Where in the world are they going with this?"

We can all avoid such confusion by prefacing our communications with a clear statement of purpose:

> *HERE'S A STARTER KIT:*
>
> - *Written emails—"I am writing today in order to…"*
>
> - *One-on-one discussions—"I would like to address…"*
>
> - *Small-group meetings—"The primary purpose of this meeting is to…"*
>
> - *Public speaking—"The purpose of tonight's talk is to…"*

Carefully articulating your purpose helps you highlight your primary objective so that everything you say afterward supports that objective and other parties can maintain their own focus.

Develop a back-up objective, left unstated initially, that you can achieve if some obstacle keeps you from reaching your primary aim. Too often we view our objective as a win-lose paradigm, one in which we either attain our goal or fail completely. In other words, as Frank Sinatra famously crooned, we want "all or nothing at all." Best to have a secondary goal in the back of your mind from the outset in order to avoid the "nothing at all" outcome.

MINI STEPS TO SUCCESS

1. Develop a primary objective for every communication.

2. State that objective at the outset of the communication.

3. Confirm, both visually and verbally, that the other party understands your objective. Try saying, "Is there anything that you would like to add to that or change?"

4. At the first sign of straying off course, come immediately back to your objective.

5. Have a secondary or fallback objective in mind in case you fail to achieve your primary objective. Half a loaf is better than no bread at all.

6. In a face-to-face encounter, end the conversation by referring to the objective. ("We had hoped to achieve agreement on this matter. Are you satisfied that we are on the right track?)

————THE TAKEAWAY————

There is a reason you are talking with someone, or participating in a group discussion, or speaking publicly. Clarify that reason in your mind and then share it with your group or communication partner so everyone is on the same page.

II

ONE-ON-ONE
COMMUNICATION

You talk about people that you don't know,
You talk about people wherever you go.
You just talk, talk too much.

—songwriters Reginald Hall and Joe Jones,
"You Talk Too Much"

9

DON'T BE A CHATTERBOX: THE 80/20 RULE

MY BROTHER-IN-LAW Steve has a name for people like this: wind merchants. But they are also known as windbags, chatty Cathys, and motor mouths. Whatever we call them, I have little tolerance for wind merchants, and I bet you are not overly enamored of them either.

This is where the old 80/20 rule comes in. It states that 80 percent of results come from 20 percent of causes. Applied to talking, it means you should try to do no more than 20 percent of the talking and no less than 80 percent of the listening when speaking with an individual or participating in a small group.

Just as you do with complex written missives, you need to minimize unnecessary paragraphs, sentences, and words in speech. Strive to say as much as possible in the fewest words. Ask more questions. Let the other party meander if they wish; learn to listen and absorb messages effectively.

Responding to a question requires a special application of the 80/20 rule. People are often too wordy with their answers. Respondents tend to say as much as they can on a matter, hoping to get points for "thoroughness." Yet it is far more effective to get right to the point and conclude with, "Does that answer your question?"

MINI STEPS TO SUCCESS

1. Every day practice saying as much as you can in as few words as possible. Practice all day long, every time that you find yourself speaking.

2. Develop the habit of letting the other party continue talking, even when they are violating the 80/20 rule. And try not to interrupt.

3. Don't be afraid of silence. After you have said what you wish to communicate, simply stop and wait for the other party to chime in. Invariably silence is golden.

4. See the forest not the trees. The more you say, the less emphasis there will be on your important points. In order to get your key messages across, do not obscure them with irrelevant blabber.

5. Use verbal cues to participate in conversations without taking over. Short comments such as "I see," and "go on," or even "yes," will engage you in the discourse without your exceeding the 20 percent mandate.

——THE TAKEAWAY——

The 80/20 rule is unlikely to work well for you unless you consciously practice applying it every day. Remember, few people enjoy communicating with a wordy, dominant, boring individual.

Most people do not listen with the intent to understand;
they listen with the intent to reply.
—Stephen R. Covey,
The 7 Habits of Highly Effective People

10

MASTER THE ART OF PROACTIVE LISTENING

MANY PEOPLE, perhaps most, deem themselves good listeners. Whoa, Nellie. Hold your horses. Few actually are. A good listener should know when and how to slip into listening mode, convince the other party that they are being heard, and process, rather than simply hear, what others are saying.

It helps to start with a perpetual commitment to actively listen. All day, every day, you should clearly focus on what other people are saying. At first, such an intense focus may appear strained or awkward. In time it will become your natural mode of listening.

Do not underestimate the benefits of maintaining an active and erect posture. I have learned that I tend to focus better, and thus be more attentive, when I am sitting up or standing straight. Conversely, I am usually poorly focused when I slouch or am otherwise unduly relaxed. Good posture invariably helps you process information better and gives others greater confidence that you are interested in their information.

Good listeners should actively prepare to listen. That is, tell yourself that you are going to listen closely and apply techniques that seem to work for you (e.g., focus on eyes, nod your head, interject verbal cues as described in Chapter 9).

MINI STEPS TO SUCCESS

1. Realistically assess your listening skills and develop a plan to make them even better.

2. When engaging in any oral communication, immediately switch into listening mode.

3. Adopt a series of verbal cues that work for you ("I see" or "yes"), phrases that help you slow the other party down, so you can better absorb their message.

4. Assess your body language when you listen, and modify it so it signals an attitude of positive engagement.

5. Learn to process the information given, rather than simply listen to what's being said; don't be afraid to ask for clarification when necessary.

6. When it's realistic, take notes for your records. That will reinforce to the other party that you are really listening to them and are interested in what they are saying. Active note taking also greatly enhances one's ability to focus.

Don't simply assume you are a good listener. Evaluate your skills realistically, and develop habits that make you an extraordinary listener. Learn to process and interpret rather than simply listen.

Those who question and probe and debate are heirs of the apostles just as much as the most fervent of believers.

—historian and biographer Jon Meacham

11

PROBE WHEN APPROPRIATE

THE ABILITY TO PROBE is an essential ingredient of success in numerous professional endeavors, including medicine, law, and sales. Simply put, probing is following up on a statement by requesting greater specificity. For example, a physician often can't genuinely understand their patient's concerns and symptoms without digging to a deeper level. An effective trial attorney is invariably a strong questioner. And a budding salesperson is well advised to uncover a prospect's real needs, concerns, and buying signals.

There are plenty of reasons to ask questions in our personal lives as well. As parents, do we not need to probe in order to determine what our children are up to? And a romantic relationship is doomed to failure if either party has an insufficient grasp of their partner's feelings.

Classic probes include "could you tell me more," "why do you feel this way?" and "what do you mean by…?" These probes may be followed up with additional ones, at least until we get to the bottom of the issue. Indeed, to be effective, you shouldn't give up until you obtain all the potentially available information you need. Most probes should end with "Is there anything else that might be relevant?"

MINI STEPS TO SUCCESS

1. Certain words and phrases suggest a follow-up probe might be necessary. Don't be satisfied with general or abstract words like "happy," "concerned," and "quality." Try to get at a greater level of specificity.

2. Have a list of phrases ready to use on such occasions, ideally phrases that come naturally to you. For example, "please tell me more," or "could you elaborate on that" are good additions to your lexicon.

3. Always be in probe mode when listening to others. Literally sit on the edge of your chair with ears pricked for an answer that will require a deeper dive. If you hear one, dive right in.

4. Never stop until you are confident that you have extracted all the information that is relevant to your conversation.

——THE TAKEAWAY——

Do not let a vague statement go unchallenged without a probe (or multiple probes). Try to get to the bottom of every issue.

Too many teardrops, for one heart to be cryin'
Too many teardrops for one heart to carry on
—songwriter Rudy Martinez, "96 Tears"

12
ASK APPROPRIATE QUESTIONS

WHEN I WAS LITTLE, my mother liked to chide me with the aphorism, "A silly question deserves a silly answer!" I guess I asked her a lot of silly questions, but I believe that is better than not asking any questions at all.

Questions are the heart and soul of almost any serious discussion. Yet asking a question for its own sake rarely accomplishes anything. Better to query in a manner that elicits meaningful and relevant information, one that will keep your communication on track.

HERE ARE SOME RULES OF THE ROAD TO HELP YOU FRAME QUESTIONS APPROPRIATELY:

- *Keep your questions short and to the point.*

- *Whenever possible, express a question in context: "So I can better help you, could you please explain…?"*

- *Do not ask two or more mini questions as part of a single question or you run the risk that the other party will overemphasize or respond to only one of the question's components.*

- *Probe in order to get the most specific and complete response to your question. (See Chapter 11.)*

- *Do not be a know-it-all. Structure your questions with qualifiers: "It appears to me that ..."*

MINI STEPS TO SUCCESS

1. Think of the art of asking questions as the third leg of a communication triad: ask questions, listen intently, probe as needed.

2. Avoid closed-end questions (questions that elicit yes or no answers). Strive for in-depth open-ended responses. Instead of "Are you satisfied with your current situation?" ask, "What needs to be done to improve your current situation?"

3. Rarely, if ever, offer your own thoughts or preferences within a question or follow another party's answer with your own opinion.

———THE TAKEAWAY———

Asking meaningful questions is the key to understanding another person's point of view and obtaining the information you need. Effective questioning is an art that can be mastered with practice.

Forget it, Jake. It's Chinatown

—closing admonition to Jack Nicholson in Chinatown

13

QUALIFY, ALWAYS, ALWAYS QUALIFY

A CENTRAL THEME of the classic 1974 noir movie *Chinatown* is that things are not always as they appear. That is so true, so often. Yet we live in a world that is frequently viewed through a lens of black and white, right or wrong, true or false. Win or lose. In fact, however, very little is 100 percent certain.

A basic rule for effective communicators is to recognize and speak to nuance. Avoid representing opinion as fact. Leave yourself wiggle room. Don't push the other party into a corner. Don't be a know-it-all-ski. Show humility.

During my 31 years as president of RYAN Associates, I either wrote or reviewed virtually every one of the 800 or so consulting reports we provided to our consulting clients. Central to these reviews was my scrutiny for any sentence that did not leave us room for error or misinterpretation. The same can be said for my verbal communications, whether they were one-on-one conversations or presentations to a group.

No one is always right. Care should be taken to use qualifiers to tone down recommendations and advice to others.

MINI STEPS TO SUCCESS

1. Fill your communications with qualifying phrases that allow you a little leeway. Expressions like "in my opinion," "from what I have seen," "if I were you," or "reportedly," all add room for nuance or some unexpected occurrence. They should be part of your everyday vocabulary.

2. Designate a full day to listen to others, either in person or through live and/or social media. Note how often others posit opinion or hearsay as fact. If you are in the mood for extreme examples of this, pay attention to virtually any politician speaking on cable or network news these days.

3. The next time you write an email, letter, or professional report, review it for statements that should be qualified. If you find any, modify them with a phrase that fits the tone and style of the document.

4. The next time you have a significant conversation with someone, be it a family member, colleague, or someone you are negotiating with, commit to qualifying any statement that is not backed up by indisputable fact. Think about your performance following the conversation and learn from your experience.

——THE TAKEAWAY——

Other than mathematical certitude (e.g., 2 + 2 = 4) and death, nothing is certain. Qualify your thoughts and suggestions accordingly.

What's your name? Is it Mary or Sue?
What's your name? Do I stand a chance with you?
*—lyricist Claude Johnson, "What's Your Name"**

14

ESTABLISH A BOND: USE THEIR FIRST NAME

DURING MY TENURE at Ryan Associates, I was front and center at 31 national conferences and scores of training courses that we held over the course of the company's life. On the flight to each conference and before I turned in each night, I studied our registration list, memorizing names and associating individuals with organizations, hometowns, and job functions.

The next day I would double down by making sure to catch at least a fleeting glimpse of a person's name on their name tag. Guess what? People were continually amazed and impressed that I knew their name and where they were from. The practice allowed me to forge a connection with people right away.

Using someone's first name in a conversation tends to establish a useful degree of comfort between you, and comfort is a key ingredient of all effective and positive communication in human relationships.

Caution: Be careful to not overdo it. Using that first name too often will come off as contrived or boorish. The point is to show you know and care about someone.

---

*This was made famous by Don and Juan and heard frequently on "Music with Mike" on WOKK radio around 1962.

Of course, last names may be more appropriate for those in a certain profession. Dr. Shultz is Dr. Shultz, not Russ, and Monsignor David Webb is Monsignor Webb, not Dave.

MINI STEPS TO SUCCESS

1. Develop a system that facilitates the learning and retention of people's first names. It could be a memory trick. ("Sam" can be "Sam I am"; Albert can be "Prince Albert.") Studying a name list in advance or maintaining a photo/name record file on your devices would also work.

2. If you do not know or if you forget a person's name, do not be afraid to ask. "Excuse me, but I do not recall your first name" is perfectly acceptable and shows you care.

3. Look a person squarely in the eye as you enunciate their first name. Strong eye contact reinforces the moment.

4. When a person tells you their name, try to repeat it right back to them (e.g., "Nice to meet you, Michael"). It's another eye-to-eye moment.

5. Continually strike a balance between using a name too often and not using it enough.

———THE TAKEAWAY———

Go to great lengths to learn and remember someone's first name, and then use it to address them. It strengthens your connection with individuals and enhances the quality of your communication.

The greatest griefs are those we cause ourselves.
—ancient Greek playwright Sophocles

15

AVOID USING NEGATIVE WORDS OR BEING TENTATIVE

ROLE-PLAYING was a key component of the scores of sales and marketing training sessions I conducted for RYAN Associates between 1988 and 2015. It never ceased to surprise me that so many young professionals tainted their mock presentations with weak, uninspiring, or negative comments.

Classic negative words include "problem," "weakness," or "concern." Each of these—and most other—negative words can be easily replaced with an active positive word that will maintain the original word's meaning but with a positive, encouraging bent. For example, all three of the words above can be recast as "opportunity."

In general, avoid calling attention to a negative occurrence. The other party may not have the same perception or may even view the situation in a neutral or positive light. Why bring negativity into a discourse if it is unnecessary?

Also avoid appearing tentative. Rather, strive to be positive, self-confident, and in control. Phrases such as "perhaps we can" or "it might be possible" should be replaced with humble yet assertive phrases. Try using "I recommend," "I suggest," or "if it were me."

MINI STEPS TO SUCCESS

1. Monitor your choice of words, both verbally and in writing. For example, you might record and critique your side of a few telephone calls, review some of your recent writings, and examine the last few weeks of outgoing emails.

2. Do you notice any patterns? Are there negative words that come up frequently?

3. Find a suitable positive word or phrase that can replace each of the negative words or phrases that you tend to use.

4. Review others' communications. Turn on virtually any cable television channel. Attend a speech. Take a class. In each instance, jot down every negative word you hear or read and later identify a positive word or phrase that could be substituted. Your personal choice of words is likely to improve accordingly.

5. Proof everything you write with a keen eye for negative words or phrases. Replace them right away. Never let a negative word survive your scrutiny.

———THE TAKEAWAY———

The turn of a single word can transform an off-putting negative statement into an active, encouraging one without changing its meaning. Emphasizing positivity will pay considerable dividends, but it invariably requires preparation, self-monitoring, time, and patience.

I'm a loser, I'm a loser
And I'm not what I appear to be
—Beatles John Lennon and Paul McCartney, "I'm a Loser"

16

STRUCTURE A PROPOSITION AS A WIN-WIN

OH, THE MISERY that comes with being a "loser." I bet you would much rather be a "winner." But true wins seldom come in one-sided isolation. Far better to view your world as a series of win-win propositions in which both parties give a little something in order to get a little something. Consider what the other party stands to gain, and structure any proposition as a legitimate win-win.

It makes so much sense to continually position anything you propose to someone else with the "what's in it for them" axiom in mind. But beware of false narratives. Your win-win needs to be legitimate.

Creating visions for win-win scenarios requires building blocks. At first it may be difficult to get beyond your parochial space. It may be easy to nail down the win proposition on your end of the equation but defining the other side's win is often elusive. Have faith all ye skeptical readers. Making a list of goals on your side and potentially those of the other party is a way to start. After enough practice in hypothesizing win-win scenarios, you will more easily envision what the gain would or could be for the other party.

MINI STEPS TO SUCCESS

1. Make a list of 10 things that you would like from your professional and/or personal contacts. Because you apparently want each item, an automatic win is built in on your end.

2. For each of the 10 wants, list what you feel is in the transaction, either tangible or implicit, that might also be a win for the other party. You will soon be able to envision your professional and personal goals as a series of win-win opportunities.

3. For each of the other party's win propositions, think of words or phrases that best describe their opportunity. Be brief, concise, compelling, and legitimate. Coming up with the win proposition is critical, but so is the ability to couch that opportunity in compelling, realistic terms.

4. Do not assume that you know exactly what appeals to the other party. Be prepared to alter your perspective midstream if their goals don't conform to your ideas.

——THE TAKEAWAY——

Remember the inherent wisdom of always thinking what's in it for the other party, and never seek an arrangement that is not actually attractive to them.

This Hollywood big shot is going to give you what you want.
I'm going to make him an offer he can't refuse.

—Marlon Brando in The Godfather

17

NEGOTIATION: A CRITICAL FORM OF COMMUNICATION

IT WAS OCTOBER 2003, during my company's 17th annual national conference in Washington, DC. A nearby water main broke in the wee hours before the conference's last day. Hotel flooded, electricity out, unshaven men and unkempt women everywhere. The hotel kitchen inoperative. Utter chaos.

The show went on. A high-profile occupational health expert gave his talk standing in water up to his ankles. An iconic Chicago-area physician made his presentation under a skylight in the hotel lobby.

A week later I spoke with the hotel's general manager to negotiate a settlement. He asked how much I wanted deducted from our final bill, and I quickly said, "$10,000." He responded in a nanosecond, "No problem." I retreated into my colleague Karen's office lamenting, "Oh, my God. I just violated my number-one rule of negotiation: Always make the other party commit first."

Never again.

Not all negotiations involve hotel floods. Have you ever purchased a car? How about a house? If you have—or plan to have—a spouse or partner, it's a good idea to polish your negotiation skills *ahora,* if not sooner. Negotiation with offspring, from toddler to adult, occurs with regularity.

Negotiation is an art that few practice effectively. Yet the rules are simple, if you adhere to them the way an insect adheres to flypaper.

CERTAIN RULES USUALLY APPLY:

- *Start beyond a negotiating position where you ultimately want to settle. You are then in position to negotiate down to your real expectation.*

- *Don't overplay your hand. Stay within reasonable demands from the outset, so you do not jeopardize your credibility.*

- *Have your win-win proposition in mind before you begin.*

- *Remind the other party about the win-win. You can even use that exact phrase: "It seems to me that $x is a fair win-win resolution."*

- *And, of course, never, ever, be the first party to make an offer.*

MINI STEPS TO SUCCESS

1. Begin any negotiation by showing sincere appreciation and respect for the other party. ("Mr. GM, your hotel is fabulous, and you did a wonderful job.") Be honest; genuinely look for things that are good and praise them.

2. Offer a carrot to the other party as an incentive for negotiating in good faith. ("Mr. GM, we really look forward to returning to your hotel in the future.") With a potential additional contract in the offing, Mr. GM is more likely to cut you a little slack.

3. Roll out your win-win in order to show that your desired resolution is favorable to both parties. ("Mr. GM, I view this is a fair win-win for each of us. Whatever the adjustment is, it will likely be offset in future revenue for your hotel.")

4. Never make it personal by casting blame on the other party. ("Mr. GM, I realize that the flood was beyond your control and that sometimes things just happen to the detriment of your guests.")

5. Always, always, always let the other party go first. Their offer may be better than your expectation. (Hint: go with the flow.) If it isn't, negotiate toward your position.

6. Negotiation is not a winner-take-all sport. Give up a few little things if it helps you achieve your larger negotiation objective and permits the other party to save face. After all, it really isn't about winning but executing a genuine win-win transaction. (See Chapter 16.)

The art of negotiation is simple if you adhere to a few basic principles. Like it or not, we all are involved in negotiations with multiple parties every day; things work better when we strive for resolutions that are in everyone's best interest.

*It is in the nature of the human being to seek
a justification for his actions.*

—*Aleksandr Solzhenitsyn,* The Gulag Archipelago

18

WHY SHOULD THEY?
ALWAYS ASSOCIATE A WHY
WITH YOUR WHAT

IN MOST NEGOTIATIONS one inevitably utters a phrase that includes a "you should" never. After all, inherent in any negotiation is a desire to achieve a certain result, and at some point in that negotiation you will need to push the other party, or even ask for something outright. Your ability to persuade the other party to align with your way of thinking is critical to your success.

It helps to associate every ask, or "what," with its corresponding "why." That way, no "you should" never stands alone; it's linked to a "why." For example, "You should brush your teeth more often, Nikko," is better as: "You should brush your teeth more often, Nikko, so you can avoid all those painful cavities."

The "why" should directly follow the "you should," either in the next breath or the next sentence.

After a while, the what-why connection will become part of your communication process. Never suggest or offer advice to someone without explaining what the advantage would be to them. Remember the cherished sales acronym: "WIIFM," or "what's in it for me?" WIIFM needs to be part of your strategic thinking and a consistent thread in your communications.

MINI STEPS TO SUCCESS

1. Never think of a "what" suggestion without simultaneously associating a "why" with it. Be certain your explanation of the "why" has merit, however. A foolish or disingenuous explanation will be counterproductive.

2. Be an advocate for the other party's perspective. What do they really want or need, and how are you going to help them get it?

3. In a face-to-face communication, do not assume the other party understands and embraces your "what-why" connection. Follow it up by asking if they agree with your proposition, and, if not, probe to determine their concerns.

———THE TAKEAWAY———

Never suggest a "what" without explaining the rationale (the win-win proposition) of your suggestion in the next sentence. The practice will strengthen your professional relationships and may make your home life easier as well.

They call me the wanderer, yeah the wanderer
I roam around around around
—*lyricist Ernie Maresca, "The Wanderer"*

19

STAY ON MESSAGE

OH, THOSE WANDERERS. They drive me C-R-A-Z-Y. One second they're here, the next second they're there, and a second later they are… Well, you get the idea.

Staying on message is seldom easy. There is frequently a temptation to throw in a sidebar or an offhand comment. Sometimes those may even include useful information. But most human minds can tag along with meanderers for only so long. When your listener or reader gets distracted, they may never get back on track with you. Game over.

You cannot stay on message if you haven't pinpointed what that message is. What exactly are you hoping to get across? How will you measure success? Once you have zeroed in on your objective and sketched a path to achieving it, you will be able to focus on the finish line.

Meandering is not the sole province of the speaker or writer. The other party may meander as well, regardless of your measured focus. Be patient, but pivot back to your message as quickly as possible.

MINI STEPS TO SUCCESS

1. Clearly define your communication objective. It may be as simple as a "yes" or a "no" response to a

proposal, or it may be a request to collaborate on a complex transaction.

2. Identify how you wish to reach your objective; define the type of communication that best serves that end.

3. Do not let others' lack of focus throw you off track. Accept such distractions with grace but strive to get the interaction back on the rails as soon as you can.

4. Use smooth, nonconfrontational transition language to return to the subject (e.g., "getting back to my point").

5. If you do have a single focus, refer to it in your introductory remarks and your summary. ("The purpose of my call is…" and, "to summarize….")

6. If you are communicating by telephone, keep a two-to-three-word summary of your objective on your computer screen or in some other visible spot. Similarly, when you are speaking face-to-face, remember your two-to-three-word focus.

7. If you are communicating in writing, say through an email, scrutinize the message for tangents or other meandering comments, and either eliminate them or rewrite that section to match your objective.

———THE TAKEAWAY———

Cut to your chase and take strong measures to remain there.

Eye contact is way more intimate than words will ever be.

—Faraaz Kazi, Truly Madly Deeply

20

LOOK 'EM IN THE EYE AND KEEP LOOKING

"THE EYES ARE the windows to the soul" is an ancient and wise proverb. Many people believe that we can understand another person in seconds merely by making eye contact.

Effective communication can vary with the amount of eye contact we achieve and its quality. Strive to manage consistent eye contact with the person you're talking with. But it's not enough to merely focus on that person. Be mindful of subliminal messages that you may be conveying through your gaze.

It is important that your eye contact be relaxed, natural, and warm. Do not come across as a lunatic by staring someone down. Rather, your eye contact should communicate kindness and show you have genuine interest in what the other party is saying. Don't forget to also glance away from time to time, lest you begin to resemble Jack Nicholson in *The Shining*. If you are speaking to a group, learn to efficiently and gently scan your audience, making relaxed but direct eye contact with as many participants as possible. Projecting a calm and positive presence is critical.

Remember that eye contact is a two-way street. You not only want to connect to the person you're communicating with, you need to learn how to read their eyes for clues to what they truly mean.

In your one-on-one conversations, make the other party feel they are the only person in your universe by staying focused on their eyes. I remember reuniting with a colleague who we will call "Ed" (in large part because that is his name). I hadn't seen Ed in a while and I had admired him greatly. As we shook hands, his eyes strayed beyond me to others in the room, implying that he might enjoy seeing them more than me. My admiration for Ed went kaput.

A few seconds may seem an extremely short time to connect with someone else's soul. But if we focus on making genuine eye contact, we can usually pierce someone's veneer and connect with their true self that quickly.

MINI STEPS TO SUCCESS

1. Watch the other party's eye contact during one-on-one conversations. Did they fall short? In what way?

2. Repeat the process when you are listening to someone address a small group. Is the speaker looking directly at the audience? Are they establishing eye contact with you as well?

3. Proactively develop your own eye-contact style. Find the right balance—not too intense, yet not too casual.

4. Imagine yourself with a set of blinders on, like a Kentucky Derby thoroughbred, and become oblivious of everyone and everything else in the room. Ignore distractions. For that moment, make the other person the most important thing in your life.

Everything that has a beginning has an ending.
Make your peace with that and all will be well.

—*Jack Kornfield,* Buddha's Little Instruction Book

21

APPETIZERS AND DESSERTS FILL OUT A MEAL

THE SUN RISES and sets. Tides roll in and out. Our lives and virtually every event in them seem to have organic opening and closing acts sandwiched around eventful middles.

So it goes with any form of communication. Set the tone, communicate the message, summarize.

Yet many people leave this order to chance. Jump into it, they think: Say your piece and be on your way.

Not exactly.

As we have noted, you never get a second chance to make a good first impression. The first thing someone says or writes tends to set the mood and the direction for everything that follows. Similarly, the last thing someone says often resonates more deeply and for a longer period than virtually anything that preceded those final words.

Develop a standard approach to openings and closings. Include expressions of respect and/or appreciation in your opening—such as thanking the other parties for their time—followed by a clear statement of your objective. Offer a roadmap to the ways in which your communication is going to achieve that objective.

A strong closing is essential as well. Play it out in reverse of your opening. Summarize the essence of the exchange, reiterate any follow-up steps, then restate your objective and thank the other party for their time and support.

The opening and closing segments of most of our communications will probably take less than two minutes. Yet, when done effectively, their impact is disproportionate to the time involved. Openings and closings are brief but vital and reward your detailed attention.

MINI STEPS TO SUCCESS

1. Think of any communication as a three-part composite: an opening, a middle, and a closing.

2. Recognize that your opening and closing are often more important than your middle, and, given their comparatively short length, easier to plan and execute.

3. Always open a communication with a sign of respect. ("Thank you for your invaluable time.") Clearly state your objective, and then provide a roadmap.

4. Use the other party's first name and look them in the eye, while simultaneously studying and accessing their body language.

5. Close with a succinct summary, a recitation of any "to-dos," and a final expression of respect and gratitude.

———THE TAKEAWAY———

Make your three-step process routine with a standard opening, the heart of your communication, and a classic closing. The total time devoted to your opening and closing statements are likely to consume just a small percentage of your overall communication but are often more important than everything you say in between.

Oh! I love to go out fishing
In a river or a creek
But I don't enjoy it half as much
As dancing cheek to cheek

—*composer Irving Berlin, "Cheek to Cheek"*

22

ESTABLISH AN EVEN PLAYING FIELD

IN THE 1990s I proudly served as a board member for the smaller of two local hospitals. One afternoon I was dispatched to meet with the CEO of the larger hospital in order to find ways that the two hospitals could collaborate. Mr. CEO's executive suite was unique. His desk was elevated several feet above the floor, which meant that any guest would be forced to look up at him from their humble chair.

If your game is intimidation and condensation, a set up like Mr. CEO's office would be right up your alley. (Let history show that when I asked Mr. CEO what his ideas were for interhospital collaboration, his answer was—verbatim— "to put your hospital out of business.")

So much for our Kumbaya moment.

Consider these the sacred silent triad: eye contact (see Chapter 20), body language, and body positioning. An understanding and mastery of all three is a critical adjunct to any oral communication.

Body positioning receives less attention from the average communicator than eye contact and body language, but it is no less important.

I FOLLOW THREE BASIC RULES:

- *Establish an even level of eye contact. Your eyes should not be above or below the person with whom you are speaking.*

- *When possible, eliminate any barrier between you and the other party. For example, I seldom sit behind my desk when speaking with someone else in the room. Rather, I move to the middle of the room and sit in a chair of the same or similar height.*

- *When speaking with someone face-to-face, maintain a reasonable distance between you and the other party. Or as Baby Bear would surely say, "Not too close, not too far, just right."*

MINI STEPS TO SUCCESS

1. Think of the places where you interact with others frequently (e.g., your office) and rearrange things so you may easily slip into a space or position that has you and your guest at an even eye level.

2. Eliminate any objects between you and the other party. That might include, for example, a small table, another chair, or general clutter.

3. Make sure that your eye contact, body language, and body positioning all convey the same message.

When you control the space, never take a position that signals dominance or superiority over the person you're speaking with. Consciously rearrange your room to facilitate a conversation of equals.

III

WRITTEN COMMUNICATION

Let's tighten it up now
Do the tighten up
Everybody can do it now
So get to it
We're gonna tighten up
Let's do the tighten up
—singer-songwriter Archie Bell, "Tighten Up"

23

TIGHTEN UP:
CHOP, CHOP, CHOP

BACK WHEN I was working for the RAND Corporation, circa 1978, I enrolled in a weekly in-house writing workshop. About eight weeks later I had been transformed from a woeful writer into a passable one. Lesson #1 from that course was: Say what you must with far fewer words.

Chop, chop, chop became a way of life. Write at will, eliminate extraneous paragraphs, eliminate extraneous sentences within those paragraphs, then eliminate extraneous words within those remaining sentences. Repeat the process at least one more time.

It is a forest-for-the-trees type of thing. Every unnecessary word or thought is likely to detract from your core message. After a while, verbosity is likely to completely obscure your central message.

I HAVE LEARNED THREE VALUABLE LESSONS IN
MY 40-PLUS YEARS OF DAILY WORD TRIMMINGS:

- *The more I chopped, chopped, chopped, the more*

likely I was to write efficiently from the outset.

- *The chop-chop mentality spilled over to my oral communication as well. In time, I realized I was saying what I wanted to say in fewer words.*

- *No matter how much I fine-tuned my communications, I still, to this day, tend to use too many words. Anyone out there think that you are reading this chapter exactly as I wrote it the first time around? Ha ha ha! The art of chop, chop, chop is a lifelong commitment.*

MINI STEPS TO SUCCESS

1. Whenever possible, eavesdrop on the way some people are able to say as much as possible with fewer words in both their personal conversations and group presentations. Note how many otherwise well-spoken people continually violate the chop-chop rule. Talk shows on cable television are exhibit A. These folks have been nicknamed talking heads for good reason.

2. Begin employing your new chopping skills in emails and text messages. No matter how short or unimportant, these written communications are a laboratory in which you can hone your chopping chops.

3. Scrutinize incoming emails and text messages with care, noting (usually with amazement) where and how often others fail the chop-chop test. You will

learn a great deal by recognizing other people's inefficient deployment of words.

4. Look for recurrent extraneous words and phrases and consciously eliminate them from your vocabulary. For example, I noticed I used the word "very" very, very much. Since then, I have worked very, very, very hard to eliminate "very" from my discourse.

————THE TAKEAWAY————

The heart of any communication can be compromised by excessive verbiage. Learn to write and speak succinctly by actively reducing the length of everything you write.

A proof is a proof. It's a proof. And when you have a good proof, it's because it's proven.

—former Canadian prime minister Jean Chrétien

24

PROOF AND PROOF AND PROOF AGAIN

MY SECOND BOOK—and first hardcover volume—was published in 2012. Preparing that book for distribution required that I proof it five times, word for word, punctuation mark by punctuation mark. Five times! Amazingly, I continued to find errors right through the fifth pass. I bet one or two mistakes still lurk within its covers.

Proofing your written work is not limited to books. I carefully proofread everything I write, including emails and text messages. For example, in this era of computer spell-checking, unintended spell-check-generated errors abound. Proofing goes beyond the search for obvious errors.

WHEN YOU PROOFREAD YOUR OWN WRITING, LOOK FOR:

- *Opportunities to chop unnecessary words (see Chapter 23)*

- *Paragraphs that are too long*

- *Ideas that flow illogically*

- *Ambiguities and misconceptions (see Chapter 27)*

- *A clear beginning, middle, and end (see Chapter 21)*

- *The clarity of your fundamental message*

Proofread everything at least twice. I seldom make a second run without finding additional room for change. Nothing is too short or irrelevant to send without proofreading.

MINI STEPS TO SUCCESS

1. Commit to carefully proofing every piece of written correspondence.

2. Look for common errors, such as overuse of a certain phrase or punctuation mark or the use of extraneous words, and become vigilant about avoiding such occurrences in the future.

3. Depending on the importance of your written message, consider proofing it a third or even a fourth time.

4. If you are in a professional environment, ask a colleague to proof your more important written communications. Four eyes are better than two.

5. Carefully read all incoming messages for errors. You will learn a great deal by being conscious of other people's shortcomings. When you find errors, does your opinion of the sender go down, even a tad? If so, imagine how others might react to any errors they notice in your work.

THE TAKEAWAY

Do not release anything you have written without first carefully proofing it word for word. Ever.

I hate everything about you
Why do I love you?
You hate everything about me
Why do you love me?
—Songwriters Adam Gontier, Brad Walst, Gavin Brown,
and Neil Sanderson, "I Hate Everything About You"

25

NEVER EXPRESS ANGER
IN WRITING

AS A PROUD part-Italian American (my mother, nee Dorothy Harrison, was English and Irish), I sheepishly admit to occasional fits of anger. Fortunately, such overt displays do not last long and, in my mind, are history within minutes. But I learned long ago, at times the hard way, to never express anger in writing.

The written word can last forever. These days there is no limit to how far a poorly conceived, ill-tempered email, text message, or letter may travel. Most anger-laden written messages are fueled by a short-term concern that is likely to abate or disappear by the next day or even the next hour. Best to sleep on your concern and awaken as a reasoned diplomat rather than a fighter.

ANGER CAN BE EXPRESSED THROUGH:

- *Nasty, mean-spirited, and condescending words. Purge such vocabulary from your usage.*

- *Ill-chosen but seemingly nonconfrontational*

words like "I disagree," which can put the other party on the defensive. Instead, try saying, "May I suggest another approach?"

- *Written "body language." To quote Potter Stewart, the late associate justice of the U.S. Supreme Court, "I can't define pornography, but I know it when I see it." The same can be said about written body language, by which I mean words that are not overtly angry but that seem to convey that feeling.*

MINI STEPS TO SUCCESS

1. In any setting, under virtually any circumstance, respond to irritants in a diplomatic manner.

2. When you are positioned to communicate harshly with another party, employ the "sleep on it" rule. Wait until the next day to shape a response.

3. Never express anger in front of a group. No one likes an angry person, and you are only multiplying the damage you have done to yourself by getting mad before a multitude. Self-effacing humor is more effective.

———THE TAKEAWAY———

Never express anger in writing, lest the correspondence spread beyond your intended audience or you change your mind after you cool down. Resist the temptation to react with anger immediately and sleep your way to a more diplomatic expression of concern.

More smiling, less worrying. More compassion, less judgment.
More blessed, less stressed. More love, less hate.
Roy T. Bennett, The Light in the Heart

26

EXUDE POSITIVE THOUGHTS

KNOW ANY Debbie Downers? Yep, I thought so. Know a lot of them? Yep, thought so again. Do you enjoy being with them? I thought not. You just hit my "we agree" trifecta.

Simply put, if people enjoy being with you, they are going to be more likely to focus on and embrace your message, written or verbal. Yet, so many people seem to lurk in the shadows of negativity.

LACK OF POSITIVITY CAN REAR ITS HEAD IN SEVERAL WAYS:

- *Through negative facial expressions and overall body language*

- *Through intemperate language in a correspondence (see Chapter 25)*

- *Through the tone and volume of one's voice*

- *Through negative words or phrases*

Some people may exude negativity as their fallback attitude, but it is also often the product of short-term anger. It may be a carryover from something totally unrelated to whatever you are communicating about at the moment. Perhaps a quarrel with your spouse during breakfast triggers you to shout at an innocent motorist on the way to work.

Twenty years ago, I served on the board of a highly successful health-care company in Massachusetts. At one board meeting, the company president, a great guy who remains a close friend, jumped on me (verbally, not physically) for what seemed to me was an innocuous comment. I was stunned. He pulled me aside after the meeting and apologized. "My outburst had absolutely nothing to do with you or what you said," he told me. "I was upset about something else." My response? "I've been there." Lesson learned.

The basic rule is wait out negative feelings in order to communicate during a more positive moment. Leave your bad moods—we all have them—at the door.

Assertive, pleasant communication is the best way to connect with others in both your professional and personal universe.

MINI STEPS TO SUCCESS

1. Notice any negativity channeled to you from others. In what way did you sense that the communication was not positive? Why do you think this negativity occurred? What lesson can you take from the experience as you strive to become more positive going forward?

2. Develop your own set of positivity rules. For example, you may want to proof everything you write (see Chapter 24), looking for any word or concept that may be construed as negative. Consider promising not to write or call anyone when you are upset.

3. Look for negative words or phrases that recur in your writing or speech. Find a positive word or expression that conveys the same meaning and replace the negative word or phrase with an appropriate substitute. For example, "I am concerned," can be reworked as, "I see an opportunity here to…." (See Chapter 15.)

4. Minimize angry exchanges, and do not let someone else's poor behavior be your license to react in kind. *Be the better person.*

———THE TAKEAWAY———

It has been said that positive people can inspire and influence others to think about things differently and can be infectious in a good way. Positivity is a choice and is directly related to one's ability to successfully communicate with others.

It is as clear as mud.

—a common expression

27

MAKE IT READABLE: USE NUMBERS AND BULLET POINTS

THE GREAT BOB DYLAN had it right. The times are indeed "a-changin'." People are reading less. The daily print newspaper is becoming a relic of the past. Short 30-second political attack ads have replaced well-conceived position papers. Books are being supplanted by podcasts and audiobooks.

Thus, it is paramount that you make your written work easy to read and absorb. Employ the three-second rule: If a reader cannot comprehend what you have written in three seconds, you have made it too hard for them.

The days of the Smith-Corona typewriter are so far gone, I barely remember using one. Nowadays, Word and other text-processing applications give writers a vast variety of visual options: multiple colors, numerous fonts in many sizes, plus shading, bolding, italics, and a family of different kinds of underlines, boxes, and more. Take full advantage of these tools to make your written material dynamic, visually appealing, and easy to read.

SOME BASIC IDEAS:

- *Change fonts and font sizes often. This can create visual pacing and highlight key points.*

- *Use colors. Colors break up the monotony of your text and make the page more reader friendly.*

- *Bold and italic type and underlining can also be used to emphasize key points and add dynamism to the look of a page.*

- *Boxed text may be a useful feature in making these vital points stand out.*

- *Indent or start a new paragraph often. This helps separate different ideas and makes reading easier.*

- *Be careful, however, not to make the page so busy looking that the reader loses track of what you are saying.*

MINI STEPS TO SUCCESS

1. Complete an inventory of the special artistic features embedded in your text-processing system. You need to know what tools you have at your disposal.

2. Create a presentation style that you find comfortable. Employ the tools that best suit you.

3. Experiment with different tools and tool combinations. Compare, for example, a straightforward black-and-white email with the same email tailored to reflect more pizzazz. How do they compare? Did the fruits of your labor result in an easier-to-read, more attractive communication? Be careful not to go overboard.

4. Borrowing from football lingo, employ a spread offense. Don't cramp your message. Use lots of white space.

———THE TAKEAWAY———

Make your emails and other written communication attractive and easy to follow. Use bullets, space generously, and mix colors and font styles where appropriate. Balance style with substance.

There is no greater impediment to the advancement of knowledge than the ambiguity of words.

—18th-century philosopher Thomas Reid

28

PROOF YOUR WORK FOR AMBIGUITIES AND MISINTERPRETATIONS

ABOUT 15 YEARS AGO, I responded to an email from a professional friend named Lana. Her message seemed unreasonably critical to me, so I replied to express my side of the argument. Shortly thereafter, Lana called me moaning that she had meant something quite different than what I had thought and that emails—indeed any written communications—are "so easy to misinterpret."

I learned a valuable lesson that day. When you proofread your writing, look for words or ideas that could be misinterpreted or that convey a nebulous gray area. The same can be said about the spoken word. Develop the ability to view your words through an ambiguity filter, and always clarify potentially vague points. Good old Richard Nixon was on the right track with his oft-stated preface, "To be perfectly clear...."

One way to address this potential pitfall is to say as much as you can in as few words as possible. (See Chapter 43.) In many instances the less you say or write, the less likely it is to be misunderstood. Round out a correspondence with a positive thought or thoughts. An upbeat tone makes it is less likely that the reader will misinterpret something in a negative light.

MINI STEPS TO SUCCESS

1. Choose five recent emails from your sent files, ideally important ones. Read each of them carefully. Did you notice anything that could be read as potentially ambiguous or that could be misinterpreted? How might you have said the same thing in a different manner?

2. Develop your own inventory of phrases that help qualify potentially ambiguous comments. Examples include "it seems to me," "correct me if I'm wrong," and "do you agree that...."

3. Show a little warmth in every communication, even when it concerns a serious matter. If there is an element of friendliness in your communication (e.g., "I hope you and your family are well"), it is less likely that the recipient will ascribe anything sinister or negative to your message.

4. Learn to be a good citizen when you are on the receiving end of a disturbing communication. If you hear or read something that can be interpreted in more than one way, ask the other party to elaborate or be more specific.

———THE TAKEAWAY———

Express your thoughts in a way that minimizes the likelihood that the remark will be misconstrued or taken as vague. Misinterpreted words can have dire, albeit unintended, consequences.

IV

SMALL-GROUP PRESENTATIONS

Better three hours too soon than a minute too late.
—*William Shakespeare,* The Merry Wives of Windsor

29

TIMING IS EVERYTHING: ARRIVE EARLY

I CONFESS I wasn't always punctual. Nowadays I am a punctuality freak. I manage my time carefully and try to always leave room for unanticipated delays when traveling to my destination because, if you want to get off to a bad start with another party, show up late.

Arriving early goes beyond making a good impression. It allows you time to catch your breath and review your objectives and strategy for the meeting. I frequently try to get to meetings 30 minutes early, but if the meeting is off-site, I will often stay in the car for most of that time preparing. You simply never know when an unexpected turn of events, such as heavy traffic or getting lost, will throw you off schedule.

SOME USEFUL RULES:

- *Resolve to get to both one-on-one and group meetings early. Try to arrive at in-house meetings at least five minutes before they start and at off-site meetings well ahead of schedule.*

- *Resist playing watch games. Don't try to fool yourself by setting your watch five minutes ahead of the actual time. Unless you are arithmetically*

*challenged, it is simply too easy to mentally
readjust the time.*

- *Carve out a little time before the meeting for
  a bathroom stop. That can preempt a need to
  excuse yourself later and allow you to feel more
  comfortable by washing your hands and face
  or combing your hair. Aim to enter the meeting
  relaxed, comfortable, and at your peak in energy
  and appearance.*

- *Whenever possible, research your destination
  ahead of time. Much of my professional work
  involved meetings with hospital clients in
  unfamiliar cities throughout the country. I
  frequently made dry runs from my hotel the
  night before a meeting in order to estimate what
  my morning drive would entail and eliminate
  potential confusion the next day. When it comes
  to punctuality, leave as little as possible to chance.*

MINI STEPS TO SUCCESS

1. Have a plan. Know when you want to arrive at
   a meeting and what you might do between your
   arrival and the meeting's start time.

2. Leave as little as possible to chance. When it comes
   to punctuality, a heavy dose of paranoia is a good
   thing.

3. Being available after a meeting is an excellent habit
   to get into. Whenever possible, do not be the one to

rush out of the door. You want to avoid giving the impression that your next activity is more important than your current one.

———THE TAKEAWAY———

Karen Joy Fowler, author of *The Jane Austen Book Club,* once wrote: "Arriving late was a way of saying that your own time was more valuable than the time of the person who waited for you." Message: Try to always arrive early out of respect for others and to settle down before your meeting.

Feedback is a wonderful thing. The best feedback bridges the gap between what we learned and what we need to learn next.
—School of Yule, 2015

30

ASSESS YOUR AUDIENCE AND ANTICIPATE THEIR EXPECTATIONS

I HAVE SPOKEN before groups of all sizes and am convinced that each one had a collective personality. Some groups are actively engaged; others are in perpetual snooze mode. Meeting attendees in different cities display distinctly different personalities. For example, Philadelphia audiences are (by far!) the noisiest, most demonstrative, and the most fun, whereas Seattle crowds seem to always be under the spell of a group sedative. (Granted, I have never spoken at a Seattle Seahawks home game.)

The message? Audiences are as different as individuals, and the astute communicator needs to tailor their message, and even their style, to suit the audience at hand. But short of taking a formal survey, how do you assess your audience from the start?

Answer: Jump right in. For example, if you are speaking before a group about improving public-speaking skills, begin by asking a few questions. Ask them about their expectations and their likes and dislikes.

SIMPLE "RAISE YOUR HAND IF . . ."
QUESTIONS MIGHT INCLUDE:

- *"How many of you have heard me speak or have*

read something that I have written?"

- *"Which of the three following goals is most important to you?"*
–Becoming a better writer
–Improving your one-on-one communication skills
–Becoming a more confident and effective public speaker

- *"How many of you have spoken before a group of 20 or more in the past year?*

If you have enough time and the audience is not large (let's say, less than 20), I recommend asking people to introduce themselves and share what they hope to learn from your talk. I routinely tell my audience that rule #1 is brevity and ask them to answer this question in no more than 30 seconds. I would easily sacrifice 10 minutes of my presentation time rather than be out of sync with my audience.

Asking questions at the outset isn't the only way to adapt to your audience. Learn how to observe nonverbal clues and adjust your style on the fly.

For example, I often begin presentations with my silly "Aunt Yola" joke (see Chapter 52) and have noticed that audience responses are on a continuum from uproarious laughter (yep, that's you, Philadelphia) to stone silence (here's to you, Seattle). I remain in Funny Frank mode if I'm in front of a laughing crowd and shamefully retreat to Serious Frank if I am before an unresponsive one.

MINI STEPS TO SUCCESS

1. Recognize that virtually every individual and group

is going to have their own unique personality and set of expectations.

2. Routinely assess the expectations of your audience by asking them a series of questions. Be prepared to recalibrate your presentation on the spot.

3. Learn to notice nonverbal cues from both groups and individuals and adjust your message and style as you grasp how different things resonate with them. Your ability to modify your style as necessary is critical.

——THE TAKEAWAY——

Do not assume that you already know your audience's point of view and expectations. Be certain to elicit feedback from them and continually adapt your communication to suit their needs and perspective.

Yes, I'm losing control of my body and soul
And my mind keeps on freaking out
I'm losing control of my body and soul
And my mouth don't know what it's talking about"
— songwriters Carl D'Errico and Roger Atkins, "Losin' Control"

31

IF YOU ARE IN CHARGE, CONTROL THE MEETING

I HAVE CHAIRED hundreds of meetings and participated in many hundreds more. In the process I have learned a few things as both a facilitator and participant.

The amount of time wasted at most meetings is breathtakingly high. Meetings seldom start on time as people straggle in late and straggle out early in order to address other commitments. Meeting objectives are rarely stated or stated clearly. Many meetings tend to be dominated by the biggest blowhard in the room. (Indeed, there is often competition to be the biggest blowhard.) And meandering off topic is a constant annoyance.

The effect of wasted time multiplies when multiple people are involved. Further, most meetings tend to fall short of achieving their intended objectives. What to do, what to do?

WHEN I CHAIR A MEETING, I TRY TO:

- *Offer three meeting date or hour options to those on the invitation list to achieve a preferred time consensus and minimize necessary absences.*

- *Schedule the meeting early in the day (e.g., 8 a.m.) so fewer people have an excuse for arriving late. Although I am a bit of a soft touch, when it comes to meeting punctuality, I tend to be Mr. No Nonsense. My rule is that no one will be admitted to the meeting room if they arrive late. Such a process may seem draconian, but I insist on starting a meeting at 8, not 8:11. As a result, attendees tend to take the entire meeting more seriously and, voila, the session is actually productive.*

- *Strictly adhere to an end time—a one-hour meeting is usually more than enough—and remind everyone to stay for the entire duration.*

- *Have someone else take notes so as not to be distracted. Afterward I distribute a summary of the notes via email blast shortly after the meeting. (It's a way to wow everyone with your short turnaround time!)*

- *Hand out an agenda with a starting time for each item and stick closely to that agenda. ("Time to wrap this issue up and move on.")*

- *Be certain that everyone has a chance to give their input. You can go around the table or room and ask each person to share their thoughts.*

- *Focus on the meeting objectives and cut off meandering as soon as possible. ("To get back to the central issue...")*

- *Concentrate on "running" rather than "dominating" the meeting.*

- *End the meeting with a summary of its key points, pending issues, and short-term follow-up steps. Conclude by going around the room for everyone's "final comment."*

MINI STEPS TO SUCCESS

1. Gain experience by trying to chair meetings, even small ones, as often as possible. Practice makes perfect.

2. Adapt a strong set of rules for conducting a meeting. Do not worry about offending others. You are likely to earn the group's respect by being firm and focused.

3. Mentally check off your list of meeting rules the next time you are in a meeting chaired by someone else. You will likely be amazed at how poorly it is conducted.

4. Do not overschedule meetings, if you are in charge. If eight people attend a one-hour meeting, that is eight hours of staff time, or a day's worth of billable hours. In many cases, you can accomplish just as much by encouraging input through an email chain.

THE TAKEAWAY

The productivity of a meeting is largely a function of its process. Establish a take-no-prisoners set of rules when you are responsible for chairing a meeting. Your meetings will be the bright exception rather than the tired rule.

Hell is paved with good intentions.
—a proverb attributed to Samuel Johnson, among others

32

CLEARLY STATE
FOLLOW-UP ACTIONS

I HAVE LEFT FAR too many meetings fired up, locked, loaded, and ready to execute a follow-up plan only to see it dissolve into nothing. Haven't you had this experience, too?

The expert communicator paves the way for follow-up action by defining and then helping to manage an agreed-upon set of actions.

Defining and managing follow-up is not as easy as it may seem, especially when you are part of a group. The stakes associated with appropriate actions are often high. And lackluster or no follow-up will upend any progress you made in your meeting.

To be a follow-up champion, first identify what subsequent activity is appropriate and reach a consensus on its nature and timing. Whenever you conceive of or hear a promising or necessary idea, ask the others what they believe should be the next step, and when it should take place. Strive for consensus. A follow-up plan without consensus is no plan at all.

Once you have reached a consensus on follow-up activities and their timing, shift into management mode, which begins with immediate and detailed documentation. You can amaze other parties with your turnaround time. Knock off an email on your laptop or device while sitting in your car just after an off-site meeting, or sprint to your computer if your office is nearby. The speed of your follow-up will not only enhance your credibility, but it will also reinforce a shared understanding that actions are a priority and not to be dismissed lightly.

The ideal follow-up memo should go beyond a mere to-do list. Include a tight timetable and identify who bears responsibility for each action. Do not assume anything. Be sure that agreement has been reached before scheduling dates or assigning responsibility.

MINI STEPS TO SUCCESS

1. Whenever you or your group decide to do something during a meeting, design a plan with a timetable for taking that idea from concept to completion.

2. Do not assume others will offer support for actions, that they are available, or even willing. Strive for consensus every step of the way.

3. Document and distribute the plan to all relevant parties as quickly as possible. But take the time to ensure that the plan is spelled out as clearly as possible. (See Chapter 3).

4. Set a date and a time for a follow-up review, either during a subsequent meeting, a one-on-one discussion, or by email. Do not leave a meeting without scheduling the next meeting. Many promising plans fade away without proactive follow-up.

5. Continuously revise and/or update your plan and timetable between meetings, as steps are completed and the plan unfolds.

————THE TAKEAWAY————

Most good ideas require an associated plan of execution and a date-specific timetable. Do not let a good idea wither into obscurity. Take control by defining and executing your plan with specific steps and a timetable that will move your good ideas from concept to fruition.

Come, let's stroll
Stroll across the floor
Come, let's stro-oh-oh-oll
Stroll across the floor Now turn around, baby
Let's stroll once more
*—Nancy Lee, "The Stroll" ***

33
DON'T BE AN AUTOCRAT: INVOLVE EVERYONE

SEVERAL YEARS AGO, I had the honor of chairing the monthly meeting of a local nonprofit organization. Typical attendance hovered around 25, and I worked hard to run a fair, all-inclusive meeting. When I stepped down from the position after three years, I had greater insight into what it takes to run a productive meeting in which everyone has ample opportunities to participate and contribute. I learned that a delicate balance between input and productivity is often indispensable.

WHAT I LEARNED IS THAT IT HELPS TO:

- *Advise the group that you intend to balance strict management of the meeting with as much participation as time allows, in an environment where every individual is respected and valued.*

---

* When she wrote "The Stroll," which became a hit tune for the Diamonds in 1957, Nancy Lee was an eighth grader at West Hempstead Junior High School in New York, one year ahead of yours truly at the same school.

- *Create a realistic agenda and then manage it with a strict eye to the time allotted for each item.*

- *Before moving on from one item and taking up the next, ask the group, "Are there any other thoughts on this topic?"*

- *End every agenda segment on time, saying something like, "Time is up; we need to move on," and offering a summary of where the group stands on that point.*

- *Pay attention to and follow up on nonverbal cues by participants. For example, "Kendra, you look like you might have a thought on this matter."*

- *On important matters, go around the room and ask everyone for their final thought ("not to exceed ten seconds").*

- *For a summary, suggesting a one-word-only response saves time and often yields a profound result. Try something akin to: "In a single word, what is the greatest obstacle to our team doing this project well?"*

As a meeting facilitator, you have a dual role: to ensure that the meeting runs crisply and productively and to simultaneously take advantage of the ideas and wisdom of every participant. Failure to do both will likely result in a poor meeting.

MINI STEPS TO SUCCESS

1. Embrace, rather than avoid, the opportunity to be a meeting facilitator. Your leadership has the potential to make a big difference.

2. Be up front about your style and ensure that meeting participants know that you are interested in their input.

3. Use your agenda as a tool to ensure that each agenda item is covered in a reasonable time frame. Too many meetings slog through early agenda items, leaving inadequate or no time for potentially crucial items later.

———THE TAKEAWAY———

There is an art to running a productive group meeting. Give everyone a true voice, while being certain that the meeting proceeds in a no-nonsense, tight, and professional manner.

V

PUBLIC SPEAKING
—PREPARATION

It goes on, and on, and on
It goes on, and on, and on
(turn it up, it goes on and on and on and on)
It goes on, and on, and on (on and on and on it goes)
'Cause we're all chained to the rhythm
—songwriters Sia Furler, Max Martin, Katy Perry,
Ali Payami, and Skip Marley, "On and On"

34

GET A LEG UP: STRUCTURE YOUR TALK AS OVERVIEW-CORE-SUMMARY

C HAPTER 21 addresses the need to adapt your opening-middle-closing sequence in most one-on-one communications. This concept applies to your public presentations as well.

> *EVERYONE IS ENTITLED TO THEIR OWN*
> *OPENING TECHNIQUE. YET FUNDAMENTAL*
> *PRINCIPLES APPLY:*
>
> - *Do not begin speaking if people are still coming into the room. It is better to lose a minute or two of your allotted time than be distracted by late arrivals during the crucial outset of your talk.*
>
> - *Begin by sincerely thanking your audience. ("No matter how often I speak before groups, I never lose my deep appreciation for the fact that all of*

you have come to hear me speak.")

- *Introduce yourself. Share your name, basic background, and the relevance of your experience or knowledge with your audience. Keep it in perspective. Few people like a self-centered, egotistical, "I am the greatest," huckster. Or in the words of Rick Warren in* The Purpose Driven Life, *"True humility is not thinking less of yourself; it is thinking of yourself less."*

- *State the objective of your talk.*

- *Provide your group a roadmap for how you are planning to achieve that objective.*

- *Involve the audience in some manner, both to get their juices flowing and to provide an organic transition to the core segment of your talk. (See Chapter 41.)*

The second, or core phase, is the heart of your talk. This phase should also have an embedded mini opening-core-closing sequence. Begin with information and facts, continue to an analysis of this information, and complete phase two by providing a summary of your conclusions.

The closing, or summary phase, like the opening phase, should be preplanned, if not standardized. I begin my summary phase by letting the audience know we are coming down the home stretch ("to summarize..."). Mere mention of the word "summary" tends to focus the audience so they know the end (of your talk, that is) is near and this is their last chance to pick up any information they may have missed.

Summarize key points, and gracefully thank the audience

for their attention. Conclude with a short emotional story. I have three stories that I rotate, depending on the nature of my talk and composition of the audience. My favorite is about Joe Mullin, a politician I worked for in 1984 and who ultimately lost his state senate bid. When I asked him how he felt shortly after he learned that he lost, he said, "The true test of a man is his ability to be the same person in good times as in bad." Words to the wise, and ones I will never forget. I've found them pertinent to many a presentation.

MINI STEPS TO SUCCESS

1. Structure your public speaking engagements in three parts: an opening, a middle, and a close.

2. Develop your own style but try to show appreciation and humility in your opening and end your presentation on a legitimate emotional high.

3. Recognize that even the middle or core section of a presentation has its own mini opening-middle-close sequence.

———THE TAKEAWAY———

Wow your audience with a gracious beginning and an emotional close. Both segments are vital and should be carefully planned.

Practice makes perfect. After a long time of practicing, our work will become natural, skillful, swift, and steady.

—*martial arts legend and actor Bruce Lee*

35

PRACTICE MAKES (NEARLY) PERFECT: REHEARSE

THE YEAR IS 1984. The era of Reagan vs. Mondale. Gary Hart, Donna Rice, and the good ship *Monkey Business.* The Tigers, Raiders, and Celtics are crowned champions. LeBron James, Scarlett Johansson, and Prince Harry are born. And I, Frank Leone, commit to improving my public-speaking skills.

For various reasons, 1984 was a turning point in my career. I recognized that becoming an adept public speaker would enhance my credibility and my ability to persuade others and subsequently open doors. I soon learned that practice, practice, and even more practice was the surest road to improvement.

How does one practice public speaking? The short answer is to pursue as many speaking opportunities as possible. Both professional and personal opportunities are likely to abound. You must learn to recognize them.

I was executive director of New England Life Flight at the University of Massachusetts Medical Center at the time. It was then the only aeromedical (i.e., helicopter) service in New England, and I aggressively sought opportunities to speak before first-responder groups and staff at regional hospitals. (Extra-cool perk: I could commute to these talks via helicopter!)

One notable talk was before a group of about 50 in December 1984. Just before I left to speak to this group over dinner, I learned from my wife's ob-gyn that we were expecting our first child. I could not resist announcing this to the assembled throng during my talk. When I arrived home later, I proudly told my wife, "Great news! You're pregnant, and you are only the 52nd person to know!"

Practicing public speaking involves more than embracing multiple opportunities to stand up before a crowd. It is critical to practice for each presentation. I am not a fan of the old "stand in front of the mirror and recite your talk" technique.

RATHER, I'VE FOUND IT USEFUL TO:

- *Study your material until you know it cold. Even if you plan to use audiovisuals or notes, pretend that you will not have access to such resources. In this way, you become so familiar with your material that you will have greater freedom to concentrate on delivery rather than substance and are likely to come across as more confident.*

- *Carve out time shortly before your talk for a final review of your material. Focus on the two or three most important or emotional lines of the talk and recite them aloud.*

MINI STEPS TO SUCCESS

1. Pay attention to the performance of speakers you admire. You may watch them in person, on television, or even on social media platforms like YouTube. Learn from the best.

2. Seek every available speaking opportunity. Short or long, serous or light, large group or small. It doesn't matter. The value is in the experience you will gain.

3. Take at least a little time to prepare for any talk. I have been speaking publicly for more than 35 years, and I invariably fall short when I fail to heed this rule.

4. Ask someone to videotape a few of your presentations. Review the videos carefully, looking for any way in which you might improve. This ritual never loses its importance. Periodically repeat the video-review technique, no matter how strong a speaker you become.

——THE TAKEAWAY——

Everyone can improve their public-speaking skills. Proactively seek speaking opportunities and be sure to get a firm command of your material prior to every presentation.

An ounce of prevention is worth a pound of cure.

—time-honored proverb

36

MINIMIZE TECHNICAL DIFFICULTIES: PREPARE FOR ANYTHING THAT MAY GO WRONG

HAVE YOU EVER attended a talk where audiovisual support or other technical aspects went haywire? No matter how effective the speaker was, the fallout undoubtedly cast a pall on the entire presentation. In many instances, such malfunctions could have been prevented or the degree of their disruption curtailed.

Prepare for the worst. Begin your technological surveillance by developing a checklist of all your support needs and thoroughly review it at the site of your talk. Do this well before your scheduled starting time.

Test every piece of equipment (e.g., laptops, projectors, cameras, audio and/or video aids) to ensure that it is working properly, whether it is your own or borrowed from the event host.

- *Have a plan to instantly replace any equipment that might malfunction midstream. For example, I routinely have backup projector bulbs and spare batteries on hand when I am speaking. Ensure that a backup laptop, loaded with relevant information, is also available.*

- *Check the degree of noise that seeps in from nearby rooms and have a contact person who can act as a go-between in case the noise becomes a problem.*

- *Keep extra copies of everything, such as a power-point presentation or handout material, on a separate disk.*

- *Assign responsibilities to staff or contacts for addressing emergencies that may arise. When I spoke before large groups, I tried to have a staff member sit in the first row so I would be able to call out to them at a moment's notice. ("Donna Lee, could you ask someone to reduce the room temperature?") Similarly, ask another staff member to stand in the back so they may be on alert for other issues that require attention.*

- *Embrace any deep concerns you may have. ("Anything that can go wrong could go wrong.") In a public-speaking context, there is absolutely nothing wrong with a little paranoia.*

MINI STEPS TO SUCCESS

1. Accept that mechanical things and modern technologies break down. Do not assume that you are entering calm, steady waters.

2. Inspect relevant equipment and technological support no less than an hour before you speak. Create a checklist and check each item off before every presentation.

3. Assign responsibilities to staff or personnel from your host venue to monitor different components of the environment and technology, such as sound, lighting, overcrowding, and ambient noise. Identify a go-to person to take care of every potential malfunction.

4. Maintain full view of these people from the podium so you may signal them if necessary.

———THE TAKEAWAY———

Managing your technological support involves both minimizing issues and establishing a plan for addressing problems when they occur.

Distractions, like butterflies are buzzing 'round my head.
When I'm alone I think of you
And the life we'd lead if we could only be free
From these distractions.

—composer Paul McCartney, "Distractions"

37

PREPARE FOR THE UNPREPARABLE: PRACTICE WITH DISTRACTIONS

I HAVE LOVED college basketball my whole life. When I was a teenager, my favorite Christmas present was an annual outing to the Holiday Festival college basketball tournament at the old Madison Square Garden in New York City. College crowds are generally loud and boisterous and will do everything they can to distract the players of a visiting team.

No wonder, then, that astute college basketball coaches often simulate distractions in their final practices before heading to a hostile gym. They pipe in loud noise, have people jump up and down in front of their team's players when they practice shooting free throws, or simply yell nasty comments like, "You're ugly, Jones!"

Whether you are preparing players for a game, training soldiers for war, or readying yourself for a public presentation, any situation that mimics a hostile real-world environment is useful.

Short of asking your 20 closest friends to jump up and down in your sightline as you practice your talk, what might you reasonably do to prepare to navigate the traffic on

Distraction Avenue?

- *Try to speak while a television is on high volume.
  Better yet, tune the television to the cable station
  that runs programming counter to your political
  preferences. If you can ignore these misguided
  talking heads, you have the chops to ignore anything.*

- *Look toward the television set as you are
  speaking. Teach yourself to ignore any movement
  that crosses your field of vision.*

- *Have someone turn off the lights for 15 seconds.
  At our 1988 national conference, the ballroom
  lights went out when I was speaking before several
  hundred people, and I simply kept on speaking.
  What was the alternative, a group nap?*

- *Have someone call your mobile phone while you
  are practicing. Train yourself to gracefully turn it
  off without skipping a beat. Of course, this could
  never happen during a real presentation. Ya' think?*

MINI STEPS TO SUCCESS

1. Distractions, interruptions, and unanticipated turns
   of events are inevitable. Build immunity to them
   through practice.

2. Develop a mental checklist of things that have a
   reasonable likelihood of creating a distraction before
   every talk.

3. Find a way to simulate these plausible distractions.

4. Have a family member or professional associate do all they can to annoy you.

─────THE TAKEAWAY─────

Things are seldom perfect. Prepare for potential distractions by simulating and working through these obstacles. Strive to be unflappable when speaking before groups.

Sleep, sleep, sleep
How we love to sleep.
—*songwriter Earl Lebieg, "Sleep"*

38

PLAY TO YOUR BIORHYTHMS: EAT, SLEEP, AND SCHEDULE ACCORDINGLY

A T THAT PESKY 1988 national conference, I was about to speak in front of the full group of about 400 people, when I impulsively gulped down a Coke for a last-minute boost of energy. Unfortunately, the rapid gulping gave myself a case of the hiccups just as I started to talk. Hic! It was out with the Coke and in with bottled water for the next 30 years.

Coulda shoulda known better. Earlier that year I held a daylong seminar in Detroit and had taken in a baseball game at the old Tigers Stadium the night before. For some reason I drank a jumbo cup of Diet Coke with a predictably nauseating Tiger Dog and found myself lying awake all night. By 4 a.m. I had given up all hope of falling sleep and somehow, some way, spoke my way through the following day.

All my caffeine-induced traumas led to a habit that has worked well for the rest of my career: *Do everything you possibly can to prepare your body for peak performance.*

> *BASED ON THE NEED FOR THAT KIND OF PREPARATION, HERE ARE MY SUGGESTIONS:*

- *Whenever possible, schedule talks at a time of day when you are normally at your best. In my case, the best time is usually early in the morning (unless I happen to be in Detroit).*

- *Do your best to maintain a normal "early to bed, early to rise" rhythm in the days preceding an important talk.*

- *If you are dealing with time-zone issues, as I often did, ignore them. That sleepless night in Detroit did serve a useful purpose: I never again really worried about not getting enough sleep. If I managed to perform well on absolutely no sleep in Motown, how detrimental could only a few hours of sleep be?*

- *If you are speaking shortly after lunch, eat as little as possible, if at all.*

- *Limit caffeine. Caffeine is possibly good for a short-term spark but, as I learned, can easily cause longer-term problems.*

MINI STEPS TO SUCCESS

1. Know your biorhythms. At what time of day are you most energetic and mentally sharp?

2. Sleep well, but do not let a fear of insufficient sleep be a problem.

3. Watch what you eat and drink prior to your presentation. An empty (or near-empty) stomach is preferable to a full or volatile one.

4. When speaking, keep a glass or bottle of fresh water within reach. If you are thirsty during your talk, water is best.

──────THE TAKEAWAY──────

Actively prepare to be at your best when you speak. Eat sparingly and sensibly. Get a good night's sleep. And, by all means, avoid those "big gulp" sodas.

I can see clearly now the rain is gone
I can see all obstacles in my way
Gone are the dark clouds that had me blind
It's gonna be a bright (bright)
Bright (bright) sunshiny day

—*songwriter Johnny Nash, "I Can See Clearly Now"*

39

GET COMFORTABLE: MAKE THE ROOM YOUR FRIEND

BEFORE A RACE, racecar drivers adjust their seat, mirror, and seat belt just so. A major league pitcher kicks dirt around the mound until he's comfortable on it. And a good public speaker will be well served by ensuring that the room in which they are about to speak is as compatible as possible with their speaking style.

I have spoken hundreds of times before both midsize and large groups. I invariably visited the room where I would soon speak well in advance to adjust things to my preference. Such rooms were usually in hotels or hospitals (the core constituency during my career). In the hotels, if I was scheduled to speak early in the morning, I would check the room late the night before, if during the day, at least an hour before my talk. Many times, I arrived too late, say, just 15 minutes early, and ignited a chaotic last-second rearrangement frenzy. (To the hundreds of hotel workers I have unjustly offended over the years, I herewith apologize.)

I LOOK FOR THE FOLLOWING DURING
MY ROOM CHECK:

- *Are the seats spaced in a way that is going to make the room look as full as possible?*

- *Is there enough space in the front of the room to allow me to easily move about as I speak?*

- *Are there distractions that might be eliminated? For example, soft (or less than soft) music emanating from a speaker, extraneous items (e.g., a projector cart) in my sightline, or an open door that reveals people walking down the hallway.*

- *If I am using audiovisual props such as Power Point (which I generally prefer not to use), is the equipment there and ready to go?*

- *If I am using a microphone, is it working properly, and is it a model that I am comfortable using? For example, I greatly prefer a wireless, rather than a wired, microphone.*

- *What about the lighting options? Where are the switches, and how many different lighting options are there? Who is my go-to person if we have problems with the lighting?*

- *Is there drinking water at the podium? Often a periodic swig is in order, if not necessary.*

This is the list that I developed; you should have a checklist reflecting your own preferences.

MINI STEPS TO SUCCESS

1. Inform the responsible parties of your expectations and preferences for the room well in advance of your presentation. Do not assume that your hosts will arrange things to your liking.

2. Evaluate the room at least an hour before your talk, ensuring time to redo any expectations that haven't been met (e.g., the room has inadvertently not been set up all).

3. When something preventable goes wrong at a public presentation, add it to your checklist so you may avoid the same problem in the future.

4. Know the name of both your on-site contact person and their next-in-command and find out how to immediately contact them if something goes wrong.

———THE TAKEAWAY———

Why speak in an environment that is uncomfortable when you have the leverage to change it to suit your needs? Review your speaking environment well before your talk and do not be shy about requesting changes in, for instance, the arrangement of chairs, the microphone, or the audiovisual equipment.

VI

PUBLIC SPEAKING —PRESENTATION

My mother thanks you. My father thanks you.
My sister thanks you. And I thank you.

—*actor James Cagney in* Yankee Doodle Dandy

40

SHOW YOUR AUDIENCE GENUINE APPRECIATION

CAN YOU THINK of anything more off-putting than failing to thank your audience for attending your talk? Yes, I can. How about thanking them in a forced, canned, and insincere manner? In most instances, such an attitude will leave you worse off than having neglected to express any thanks at all.

Thank your audience during both your opening and closing remarks. And do it with sincerity and humility. A thank you goes beyond the two simple words. Place the reason for your gratitude in a broader context: "I have been speaking for many years, and I never fail to appreciate the people who make time in their tight schedules to come out and listen to me."

I make a habit of looking for the best in everyone I meet and letting them know exactly what it is when I find it. Why keep it to yourself? Sharing your positive observations invariably pleases the other party and makes you feel good as well. The same rationale applies to a group of people.

There are many reasons to thank your audience. Depending on the circumstances, any of the following could warrant acknowledgment and appreciation:

- *They simply showed up.*

- *They arrived and were seated on time.*

- *They came from a long distance or overcame traffic issues.*

- *They welcomed you warmly.*

- *They were responsive during your presentation.*

You might also praise the city you are in: "Chicago is one of my favorite cities. I love the energy here, to say nothing of the great Italian restaurants. (Shout out to Carmines, my favorite Italian restaurant in the world!)"

Or you could compliment the organization hosting your talk: "I have always had a soft spot for the Rotary Club. You provide great service to the Hoosick Falls community, and I am honored by your invitation to speak."

MINI STEPS TO SUCCESS

1. Be humble and search for something to appreciate in every person and group that supports you.

2. Look for the good in everyone (or in any place or city in which you are speaking) and be aggressive in sharing those good impressions with the person or group.

3. Time is everyone's most valued asset. Thanking people for their time is a universal thank you default option.

4. Thank an individual or group at least twice—at the outset and near the conclusion of your talk.

————THE TAKEAWAY————

In an honest and humble way, let people know when you appreciate them or something they have done. This rule applies to individuals as well as groups. Bear in mind that a person's time is their most precious asset.

Here they come, here they come
Here they come, here they come
Wooden soldiers on parade

— *lyricist Ballard MacDonald, "Parade of the Wooden Soldiers"*

41

CREATE ENERGY: MELT THE ICE AROUND YOUR AUDIENCE

THE INFAMOUS wooden soldier conference: March 7, 1995. Nashville, Tennessee. More than 100 registrants were attending a special one-day conference organized by our company. It was a gloomy day outside the Nashville Marriott and, before long, inside its main ballroom as well.

We had high hopes for our featured speaker, David. He showed up with plenty of good material but a flat presentation style. Things went from poor to poorer when, oblivious of his own wooden delivery, he admonished the assembled throng to "stop looking like wooden soldiers." Bad idea, David, bad idea.

This conference was not rated well, and the evaluations of David were even worse. (What a shocker!) But I learned an invaluable lesson that day. Audiences are likely to be stone cold unless you actively warm them up.

The next time I spoke before a large group, I employed an ad hoc warm-up technique, and it worked well.

THE FOLLOWING IDEAS HAVE BEEN A
STANDARD PART OF MY OPENING SHTICK
EVER SINCE:

- *Ask the audience to think about how they would answer a certain question, especially if the question can be tied to the session's primary topic. For example, if you are about to speak about the upcoming Super Bowl, you might ask, "Who do you think is going to win the Super Bowl this year, and why do you feel this way?"*

- *Following the question, after 10 seconds or so, ask everyone to stand up. I believe you need to thaw the audience physically as well as mentally, and unexpected body movement does the trick.*

- *Ask everyone to share their Super Bowl prediction and rationale with the person standing on either side of them. This phase normally elicits laughter and an uptick in noise and gets the audience to think more about the question. Who knows, it may even result in some new friendships or romances.*

- *Tie the question everyone just answered to the upcoming theme of your talk: "Now I am going to tell you who I believe will win the Super Bowl and why." I guarantee that hardly any wooden soldiers will remain, as everyone becomes more physically energized and focused on your talk.*

- *If you pose a question that has a definite answer (e.g., "In 53 years how many non-quarterbacks would you guess were named Super Bowl MVP?"), you might add that you will reveal the number later in your talk. You may even have a few people at the edge of their seat waiting for the answer.*

MINI STEPS TO SUCCESS

1. Do not assume that your audience will be energized and engaged to begin with. Odds are they will not be, until you push the right "blastoff" buttons.

2. Play your Olivia Newton-John card and get physical. Ask your audience to stand, stretch, raise their hands, or exchange information with their neighbors.

3. Make your audience think as well as move. Better yet, make them think about the topic you are about to cover.

4. Tie loose ends together by frequently associating your warm-up question with the remaining information in your presentation.

———THE TAKEAWAY———

Don't take for granted that your audience will arrive at your talks focused and engaged. Energize the group physically and mentally by asking them to think and move right at the beginning.

KISS
(Keep it simple stupid).
—acronym coined by engineer Kelly Johnson
at the Lockheed Skunk Works

42

WHY CONFUSE THEM?
KEEP IT SIMPLE

A FEW MONTHS AGO, I attended a lecture on gut health given by a highly regarded nutritionist. She was full of useful information but seemed to float off into uber-technical tangents that left me confused and exhausted. I wrote her an unsolicited, but kind, email a few hours later, and we soon made a trade. She would tutor my wife and me on nutrition, while I trained her in public speaking. My best trade ever!

Speak in simple, clear terms. Overly technical language, especially when it's tangential, clutters the information field and detracts from your core message. This is true even when the tangents are interesting. The more complex a message becomes, the harder it is for people to remain engaged.

When it comes to great communication, more is seldom better.

HERE ARE SOME USEFUL TIPS:

- *Your remarks should be interesting and accessible to both the most and least intelligent people in the room. Such balance can be a challenge, but it's important not to bore Mr. Smart nor fly over the head of Mr. Well, He Has Other Good Traits.*

- *I learned that parenthetical explanatory comments following potentially complex words or thoughts work well. For example, I might use the word "interquartile range," and then immediately follow with, "that is, all those whose score was somewhere between the 25th and 75th percentile."*

- *Speak in verbal mini points rather than through the cadence and flow of a narrative paragraph. If your presentation were on paper, the former would look like a meeting agenda and the latter like a page from Moby Dick. The verbal mini-point presentation makes it easier to keep your message simple.*

- *Wow the audience with your message, not with your vocabulary. Multisyllable, fancy words might be impressive on a first date but are less than effective in a public presentation.*

MINI STEPS TO SUCCESS

1. Learn to speak in simple terms. It is more difficult than one might think. There is much to be gained from working to actively improve your ability to keep your messages simple.

2. Think of your public presentation as a list of points, rather than a long interlocking story.

3. Get to your key point quickly.

4. Structure your remarks in a way that can be understood and embraced by people of different levels of intelligence and life perspectives.

————THE TAKEAWAY————

Do not do anything that might detract from the focus on your core message. State what you must in easy-to-understand, simple terms, and continually reinforce your central theme.

Like all sweet dreams, it will be brief, but brevity
makes sweetness, doesn't it? Yes, I think so.
Because when the time is gone, you can never get it back.
—novelist Steven King, 11/22/63 book

43

NOBODY LIKES A MOTORMOUTH: MASTER VERBAL BREVITY

WHEN IT COMES to communication, verbosity is complexity's cousin. You not only need to keep it simple (see Chapter 42), you need to keep it brief.

Brevity often flies in the face of noble communication intentions. It is tempting to add additional information (complex or not) that might "complete the picture" or make you sound more informed. It is tempting to continue talking for fear of an interruption or out of concern that your silence will indicate weakness. But capitulating to such temptations is ill-warranted.

Assume your presentation has been scheduled for a 45-minute time block. The temptation is to plan a 44-minute talk (which you customarily rush or even cut short at the end because you "fell behind"). Most speakers do. I prefer to break my 45-minute allotment into several segments.

A SAMPLE PRESENTATION PLAN MIGHT
LOOK LIKE:

9:00 Introduction, thank audience, state
objective, provide a roadmap

9:05 Audience stand-up, question, and interactions

9:10 Core presentation

9:30 Summary and emotional closing story

9:35 Questions and answers

9:44 Final thank you

FIFTEEN MINUTES MAY SEEM LIKE A LONG TIME FOR AUDIENCE QUESTIONS BUT USUALLY IS NOT, AND THE SEGMENT CAN SERVE ADDITIONAL PURPOSES, SUCH AS:

- *a hedge against falling behind; no need to rush or truncate*

- *an opportunity to express other relevant thoughts ad hoc*

- *an additional gesture of respect for your audience.*

A strict timetable encourages brevity because you simply have less time to say your piece and, as such, need less filler. It also alleviates pressure to finish all your points, as you have a 10-minute get-out-of-jail-free card in your back pocket. You can speak more slowly and clearly.

MINI STEPS TO SUCCESS

1. Plan for the length of your core presentation to be far less than your total time allocation.

2. Bookend your core presentation with a planned opening (overview, audience activity) and closing (final story, long question/answer period).

3. Do not fear an extended question/answer period. If audience questions dry up, you can ad-lib one or more backup thoughts (prepared well in advance). As in, "It just occurred to me that...."

4. Do not fear ending the entire session a little early (but not after only eight minutes). Far better to say everything slowly and well and have excess time at the end than to rush through your material and leave your audience gasping for breath.

———THE TAKEAWAY———

Set yourself up for success by meting out your time during a public presentation in a way that condenses the time allocated for your core points. Speak slower, pare down your words, and avoid feeling rushed.

We're gonna rock around the clock tonight
We're gonna rock, rock, rock, 'till broad daylight
We're gonna rock, gonna rock around the clock tonight
—lyricists Max C. Freedman and James E. Myers,
"Rock Around the Clock"

44

IT'S ABOUT TIME: KEEP YOUR EYE ON THE CLOCK

A SEASONED QUARTERBACK is well acquainted with the two-minute drill: two minutes to go in the game, down by four, and no timeouts remaining. His team needs to score a touchdown quickly, but not so quickly that the other team has time to score.

It's called time management, and our quarterback friend may have to do it in front of a nationally televised audience with a viewership in excess of tens of millions. Think you have it hard?

Time management is no less vital for the public speaker. If you are not properly prepared to manage your time, you will likely either run out of it (rush too quickly through your material) or run out of material (finish too early).

That reminds me of the time a high-profile (but somewhat flamboyant and controversial) health-care executive served as the keynote speaker at one of our national conferences. He was scheduled to speak from 9 to 9:50 a.m., with 10 additional minutes tacked on for a question-and-answer session.

Mr. S. mastered the art of brevity alright. He concluded his remarks at 9:08 and began walking off the stage! At that moment I ran a record 10-yard dash, grabbed the nearest live microphone, and loudly asked, "Mr. S. would you mind taking a few questions?" I made up a question on the spot, then handed the mic to the person next to me and told him to ask a question, any question, as soon as Mr. S. finished answering my question. And we continued like that for 40 minutes. Phew!

Moral of the story: Do not end your talk too early.

HERE ARE SOME WAYS TO STAY ON YOUR TIME TARGET:

- *If you place your watch on the podium or on top of the nearest tabletop, you will be in a good position to sneak peeks at the time in a way few will notice.*

- *Ask a staff member to sit in the front row and flash you "5 minutes" and "10 minutes" signals (5 or 10 fingers will do).*

- *Create a few time mileposts. Know where you need to be in your presentation at, say, 9:15 a.m., and seamlessly try to evaluate if you are ahead or behind schedule.*

MINI STEPS TO SUCCESS

1. Schedule your presentation in small time blocks before you speak.

2. Bring a timepiece such as a watch or a small clock and place it in your line of sight.

3. Ask someone to be your clock-watching consigliere. They can concentrate on your time management while you concentrate on the substance and delivery of your message.

4. Above all, try not to cover too much in too short a time span. Better to finish early than rush over or eliminate a portion of your presentation.

———THE TAKEAWAY———

You cannot complete things on time if you do not have a mechanism to measure and monitor your time. Find a way to keep a gentle eye on the clock without compromising your focus.

Be sincere, be brief, be seated.

— President Franklin Delano Roosevelt

45

SHORT QUESTIONS BEGET SHORT RESPONSES: ANSWER QUESTIONS SUCCINCTLY

OCTOBER 1984. I posed a question to one of that era's most prominent politicians during a Q&A segment following a dinner event. Mr. High Profile Politician answered my question, then answered my question some more, and then continued to further answer my question while I stood next to my seat aimlessly moving my feet. He later recognized me at the receiving line and (surprise!) buttonholed me and picked up where he left off with his earlier response.

Mr. High Profile Politician is by no means alone in his wordiness when answering a simple question. Since that evening more than 35 years ago I have noticed that even polished speakers will fall into the "endless response" trap.

I have never properly diagnosed this most prevalent "loquacious response disease." Perhaps the speaker is uncertain of their answer and wishes to cover multiple bases. Perhaps they want to stall in order to reduce the time available for additional (and potentially more difficult) questions. Heck, maybe the speaker is just a chronic blabbermouth.

WHEN YOU ARE ASKED A QUESTION DURING
OR FOLLOWING A PRESENTATION YOU SHOULD:

- *Repeat the question. Perhaps some members of the audience did not hear it. Repetition provides the person asking the question an opportunity to clarify it. (There is nothing quite as silly as providing a lengthy response to a question that was never meant to be asked). The pause also gives you a little extra time to consider your response.*

- *Dive headfirst into brevity mode. Craft your response using as few words as possible. Remember that the person who asked the question may be the only person in the room who cares about the answer. Do not waste everyone's time when only one person really may be interested in your answer.*

- *As soon as you have answered the question (briefly, of course!) ask, "Does that answer your question?" If the answer is no, the same brevity rules apply for response #2. Ask the questioner if they are satisfied with your answer a second time only if you sense the rest of the audience may not be poised to ask additional questions.*

- *Plan to remain in the room following your talk. Let your audience know that "I will stay here for a while if anyone has additional questions." Such post-talk conversations can be hugely beneficial for both parties.*

MINI STEPS TO SUCCESS

1. Listen carefully when other speakers take questions from their audience. You may be surprised how often they violate the "keep your answer brief" rule.

2. Learn to monitor your own responses, keeping in mind the general level of interest in the subject.

3. Remain available after a presentation, for any follow-up questions.

——THE TAKEAWAY——

Keep your response to audience questions as brief as possible. The person who asked the question may be the only person in the room who cares about your answer.

It's not what you say, but how you say it.

—movie actress Mae West

46

AVOID MONOTONY: CHANGE VOLUME, PACE, AND INFLECTION

DR. ALBERT MEHRABIAN, professor emeritus of psychology at UCLA, conducted numerous studies on nonverbal communication and concluded that the essence of communication is 7 percent verbal and 93 percent nonverbal. Further, he discovered that about 55 percent of nonverbal communication emanated from facial expressions, gestures, and postures, while only 38 percent came from tone of voice. In other words, by Dr. Mehrabian's standard, 7 percent of your communication's impact comes from what you say, and 93 percent from how you say it.

Although one may dispute the exactness of his numbers, the point is clear: volume, pace, tone, inflection, and physical delivery are the heart of communication.

Imagine volume, tone, and pace as strings on a musical instrument. Each can play a role individually or in harmony with the other features. Every feature can flow from active to inactive, from loud to soft, in unison with another feature or on its own. Volume, pace, tone, and inflection are tools to manage in your presentations.

WHAT DOES THIS MEAN IN PRACTICE?

- *Speak in three general volumes: loud, soft, and normal. Use loud when expressing emotion (both good and bad), soft when sharing "a secret" or when you are imploring your audience to pay closer attention.*

- *If you are the same pace throughout, you will lose your audience in a heartbeat. Continually adjust your cadence from slow to fast and back to normal. Save your slow pace for your most important points and use your fast pace when you want to re-energize your audience.*

- *Match the spirit of your comments with a voice tone appropriate to that spirit. Expressing joy? Speak with glee. Calling attention to a tragedy? Speak in a somber tone.*

- *If you tend to speak in a monotone, include change of pitch in your verbal playbook. I often adjust my inflection if I notice a lull in the audience's energy, and I realize I may have slipped into a monotone. A brief change in intonation or volume will often re-engage your audience.*

MINI STEPS TO SUCCESS

1. Mix it up and at all costs avoid being Mr. or Ms. Monotone. A change of pace, inflection, or volume is the best pitch in your pitching repertoire.

2. Recognize the breadth of your presentation toolbox. You can use the volume tool, the tone tool, the pace tool, the inflection tool, or a combination of all four. Include body movement, body gestures, and eye contact and the number of permutations at your disposal goes through the roof.

3. As William Shakespeare said, "All the world's a stage, and all the men and women merely players." Polished speakers are more than speakers, they are actors utilizing the gamut of their verbal and nonverbal capacities.

——THE TAKEAWAY——

A public presentation, like many forms of entertainment, is best delivered through an ever-changing stream of volumes, speeds, tones, and inflections. Consider it a verbal version of a symphony, relying on contributions from all its sections—string, woodwind, brass, and percussion.

Silence is golden
But my eyes still see
Silence is golden, golden
But my eyes still see

—*songwriters Bob Crewe and Bob Gaudio, "Silence is Golden"*

47

SILENCE IS GOLDEN: DO NOT FEAR SILENT PERIODS

I HAVE PLAYED many rounds of golf since the age of 14 but few of them well. A classic golf principle notes that the easier you swing the golf club, the better you strike the ball. The advice may be counterintuitive and hard to follow, but it is as true as rain.

An equally true yet counterintuitive concept can be applied to embracing silence. Or, as my ninth-grade English teacher Mr. Henderson liked to quip, "Silence reigned, and we all got wet." Unfortunately for Mr. Henderson, the class got tired of his silly joke by late September.

A HEALTHY DOSE OF SILENCE:

- *Allows your audience to catch their breath and reclaim their energy in order to prepare for what's to come in the next segment of your presentation.*

- *Gives you a micro time-out in which you can begin formulating your next thoughts.*

- *Provides the audience with a moment to process what they have heard.*

- *Injects a sense of calm to the room.*

I understand why so many speakers find it difficult to remain silent. They might assume that their audience thinks less highly of them or that the audience fears that the speaker is panicking or for some reason can't speak. The audience may even think the presentation is over

None of these fears are legitimate.

I've found that audiences appreciate a little quiet. If the silence is not overly long or does not occur too frequently, you should look at a quiet moment as an opportunity to regroup and move forward.

MINI STEPS TO SUCCESS

1. Accept (within reason) that a little silence is a good thing and welcome it as an opportunity rather than a short-term concern.

2. Develop a sense for just how much silence will hit the sweet spot for your audience. For example, trial and error might suggest that six seconds of silence works best for the audiences that you normally address. Try to end the silence after that amount of time.

3. Respect the "silence is okay" principle when it is employed by others.

——THE TAKEAWAY——

Provided that it neither occurs too often nor lasts too long, silence is usually a good thing. Embrace rather than push back on the opportunities inherent in that short quiet moment.

The more you speak from the heart,
rather than thumping the agenda,
people will listen or relate,
or open themselves up more.

—actress Drew Barrymore

48

CONNECT BY SPEAKING FROM YOUR HEART

THE LATE DR. FOREST FISHER, then national medical director of the Campbell's Soup Company, was the keynote speaker at my company's second annual national conference in 1988. Because I was worrying about everything I had on my plate that day, I was barely listening when he did something that provided an invaluable lesson.

At a critical juncture in his talk, Dr. Fisher briefly placed his palm near his heart and softly whispered, "Let me speak from my heart for a moment, if I may." I noticed that everyone, yours truly included, perked up as though they had been given a shot of adrenalin.

Virtually everyone can relate to someone who speaks from their heart. Of course, the person needs to walk the walk and say something that is important to their broader narrative. Dr. Fisher's palm-to-his-heart imagery helped a great deal. I recall thinking, "He must really mean what he is about to say."

If you try this, watch your hand movement. If it comes off as contrived, phony, or overly dramatic, you have taken a step backward. Use the palm-to-heart gesture only once. Your audience will be affected by the first adrenalin shot and gain little from a second. Watch your timing, too: A gesture in the middle of a presentation helps reenergize a drifting audience. A heartfelt utterance toward the end of a talk sets the stage for an emotional close.

MINI STEPS TO SUCCESS

1. Include one (but no more than one) "from the heart" moment in every talk. Find a sweet spot during your talk or wait for what appears to be a lull in the group's energy.

2. Be certain your "from the heart" comment is central to your basic message and is based on your opinion or perception rather than fact.

3. Do not overact your palm-to-heart gesture. The movement should suggest a gentleness of spirit. It shouldn't be sweeping or sudden. If hand gestures come naturally, use them.

4. Change your pace, volume, and body gestures. Slow down and speak the words "from the heart" slower and softer than your normal cadence and volume. Gently nudge your upper body forward a bit as a sign that you are about to establish an extra special connection with your audience.

———THE TAKEAWAY———

Every audience member has a heart, and most of them are likely to perk up when they hear the phrase "from the heart." Go beyond being a robotic, coldhearted speaker to one who touches others on a human level.

Whether I'm right or whether I'm wrong
Whether I find a place in this world or never belong
I gotta be me, I've gotta be me
What else can I be but what I am

—songwriter Walter Marks, *"I've Gotta Be Me"*

49

DO NOT ACT:
JUST BE YOURSELF

HAVE YOU EVER seen a three-dollar bill? Probably not. But if you did see one you would likely recognize the currency as fake, a fraud, perhaps even an insult.

Authenticity is a key to effective communication. We are who we are, and we are playing in perilous waters if we try to be someone we are not. Yet public speakers fall into the artificial persona trap far too often. Why is this?

I suggest that many speakers assume false identities because they fear their audience will not like the real them as much as the mythical person they are portraying.

> *HERE ARE SOME THINGS TO KEEP IN MIND.*
> *IF YOU ARE NOT:*

- *inherently funny, do not try to be a comedian.*

- *flamboyant, do not try to Mr. or Ms. Personality Triple Plus.*

- *an emotional sort, do not rely on too many tearjerkers.*

- *naturally dynamic, do not try to emulate the energizer bunny.*

- *a deep thinker, do not try to be Plato II.*

Be yourself. Apply the concepts described in this section—humility, structure, audience engagement, and changes of tone, volume, and pace, to name a few—and let your natural personality rule the day.

MINI STEPS TO SUCCESS

1. Know yourself and embrace who you are, as opposed to the mythical Public Speaker Extraordinaire you might think you need to be in order to connect with your audience.

2. Identify your primary personality shortcomings and downplay them during your talk.

3. When appropriate, be humble and note who you are not: "I'll never be named comedian of the year, but I do want to share a funny story that I recently heard."

4. Continually monitor other speakers and note when they seem to exude a personality that appears different than their authentic self. Learn from these examples.

———THE TAKEAWAY———

We are each a little different from everyone else. Be comfortable in your own skin. Do not try to project a persona that is different from your true self in hopes of connecting better with your audience. Such a phony posture will be evident and work to your detriment.

Memories light the corners of my mind
Misty water-colored memories of the way we were
Scattered pictures of the smiles we left behind
Smiles we gave to one another for the way we were
   —lyricists Alan Bergman, Marilyn Bergman,
   and Marvin Hamlisch, "The Way We Were"

50
MAKE IT PERSONAL: SHARE ANECDOTES AND EXPERIENCES

WHEN YOU GET to the heart of it, aren't we all just people trying to connect with other people? Each of us has a storehouse of anecdotes, funny personal stories, and unique experiences. We usually identify with other people as we listen to their stories and vice versa. Reeling an audience in with a good story is an excellent bridge to engagement and a way of keeping them engaged while you get to the heart of your talk.

SOME RULES OF THE ROAD:

- *Ensure that your anecdote has a reasonable connection with the point of your talk. Irrelevant gibber is irrelevant gibber.*

- *Recognize that inherent humor or an underlying lesson are more useful than a story told for a story's sake.*

- *Keep your story reasonably short (two minutes max). Some in the audience may be anxiously awaiting the heart of your talk. Don't disappoint them.*

- *Engage your audience at the outset of the story. ("How many of you have ever been removed from a plane because the flight was oversold?") Such engagement will often pique audience interest, stimulate physical movement, and provide an emotional lift. (See Chapter 41.)*

MINI STEPS TO SUCCESS

1. Once you develop an outline for a public presentation, think of a humorous or meaningful story that is relevant to some aspect of your topic.

2. Use anecdotes to evoke emotion (laughter, sentimentality). Tell your stories from a common person's perspective.

3. Make a list of your best anecdotes and funny stories. Have the list handy when you are selecting an anecdote for a new presentation. Some anecdotes in your inventory may be relevant to numerous topics and a variety of audiences and can be used in different contexts.

4. Using the same story before different groups is useful. Repeating it allows you to polish your delivery.

———THE TAKEAWAY———

People like stories, all kinds of them. . . funny, emotional, even eerie or odd "you won't be-lieve this" stories. When the story provides a bridge to the topic at hand, the audience will like it even more. Pepper your talks with real-life experiences and you will more readily connect with those you're talking to.

And then there was Jimmy Two Times,
who got that nickname because he said everything twice,
like: 'I'm gonna go get the papers, get the papers.'
—*description of a character in* Goodfellas

51
REEMPHASIZE KEY PHRASES AND POINTS: REPEAT, REPEAT, REPEAT

REPETITION PLAYS a significant role in mass communication. In good ways and bad ways. In the most positive sense, repetition allows communicators to be increasingly confident that their point is being heard and understood. On the ominous side, frequent repetition of the "big lie" has long been a technique used by totalitarian movements, dictators, and other unscrupulous entities.

I prefer to focus on the good uses of repetition, while remaining conscious of the potential harm inherent in repetition.

Whether you are speaking to a large group, at a small meeting, or one-on-one, there is likely no more than a handful of concepts you want the other party to absorb. A six-pack of properly understood takeaway points or concepts is an excellent achievement.

SOME POINTERS ON HOW TO ACCOMPLISH THAT:

- *Before a talk ask yourself what four to six points you want your audience to absorb, if they absorb nothing else.*

- *Slip into repeat, repeat, repeat mode when those points come up during your talk.*

- *Repeating a "repeat point" once is good; twice is usually more emphatic. (Go beyond two repeats and you are skating on the thin ice of Lake Overkill.)*

- *Deliver your repeated point in a slower pace and louder tone and enunciate even more clearly than usual. Think of your repeated phrase or sentence as a line in your text that is printed in bold. The words should jump out.*

- *Advise your audience that you are intentionally repeating your point or points. ("This is important. To repeat....") Using the actual word "repeat" tends to get your audience's attention.*

MINI STEPS TO SUCCESS

1. Predetermine the most important points in your presentation.

2. Plan to repeat each of these points at least once.

3. Let your audience know that you are intentionally repeating a point or two because they are so important. Include the phrase "to repeat."

4. As appropriate, summarize your key points at the end of your talk.

Do not leave your audience's grasp of critical information to chance. Repeat key points once or even twice. and let your audience members know why you are doing so. In the words of Zig Ziglar, the prominent motivational speaker, "Repetition is the mother of learning and the father of action, which makes it the architect of accomplishment."

I'm funny how? I mean funny, like I'm a clown? I amuse you?
I make you laugh? I'm here to amuse you?
Whattya you mean funny? Funny how? How am I funny?

—actor Joe Pesci in Goodfellas

52

ELICIT LAUGHTER: INCLUDE ONE FUNNY STORY

OKAY, I KNOW you have been waiting (surely with bated breath) to hear my "Aunt Yola" joke since I mentioned it in Chapter 30. Great news! Your Aunt Yola ship has come in.

My Aunt Yola Squadrito (yes, that was her real name) was worried that her husband, Pep (yep, real name again), was losing his hearing. I told Aunt Yola to try the following experiment with Uncle Pep. Stand at the back of your den and call out his name. If he does not answer right away, split the space difference and try again. If he still doesn't answer, stand directly behind Uncle Pep and try one last time.

Aunt Yola got back to me a short time later: "I stood in the doorway and said, 'Pep, can you hear me?' Silence. I split the difference and tried again. Crickets. I finally stood right behind Pep and asked him one last time. And Pep responded, "For the third time, Yola, yes I can!'"

I'm not going to win the comedian of the year award, but over the years the Aunt Yola joke invariably broke the ice and was warmly received by dozens of audiences. For the record, my Aunt Yola joke was one of two "jokes" in my minuscule arsenal. I'll save the "My friend Rick's father" story for a future book.

Regardless of your speaking style, try to connect with your audience on multiple levels—as a fellow human, at an emotional level, and with some degree of levity. You do not have to be a natural comedian (see Chapter 48) to throw in a single humorous story or anecdote.

THERE ARE MANY POTENTIAL SOURCES FOR FUNNY STORIES:

- *A recent real-life experience involving yourself or someone you know. Often audience members can relate directly to such a story.*

- *Old-fashioned plagiarism. You don't really think I made up my Aunt Yola joke on my own, do you? I Googled "funny stories," and the prompt listed 2,620,000,000 resources. That's right: more than two billion resources for funny stories. I bet you can find something humorous in such a massive haystack.*

- *Something that happened that day or even walking into the meeting room. Not too long ago I was asked to introduce a speaker at a community event. On the way to the podium I noticed that I had each of my shoes on the wrong foot. Given that I have put shoes on approximately 26,663 times consecutively without such a problem, the mistake was notable, and I shared it with my audience. History will judge which was stupider— the wrong-foot act itself or my willingness to share it with everyone in the room.*

MINI STEPS TO SUCCESS

1. Include a funny quip or story early in every public presentation.

2. Realize that ample funny stories exist! You do not need to be creative.

3. Tailor the humor to your audience. For example, a "three cowboys walk into a bar" joke may not play well with an audience of neurosurgeons.

4. Maintain a small inventory of funny stories. The more often you repeat a joke the more polished your delivery.

——THE TAKEAWAY——

A little humor can go a long way in a public presentation. Incorporate a story into all your talks, ensuring that the story is, in fact, humorous and appropriate to the topic at hand and the personality of your audience.

Don't be impacted by things that are only
fleeting temporary distractions.

—*law professor Steven Redhead,* Life is a Dance

53

DO NOT DISTRACT: MINIMIZE OR ELIMINATE AUDIOVISUALS

IT SEEMS LIKE only yesterday that I was lugging a giant slide projector and carousel filled with slides into my presentations. Then the Power Point era dawned, and I only had to worry about those fragile, bulky, and expensive LCD projectors.

One problem from slide projector days did follow public speakers into the Power Point era. Speakers too often looked at their screen and simply read Power Point material verbatim while largely ignoring their audience. Guess what? The audience ignores the speaker as well, because their eyes are fixated on the screen and the very words the speaker is reading. Talk about a speaker-audience disconnect.

You must connect directly with your audience, meaning that you must have nearly constant eye contact, as well as effective engagement, with them. Toward that end, I prefer to either eliminate such audiovisual support or use it sparingly.

HOW DO I DO THAT? HERE ARE SOME TIPS:

- *Whenever possible, avoid using Power Point slides; words on a screen tend to distract from your presentation, rather than enhance it.*

- *In some cases, you really do need visual support (e.g., for statistical data or graphs). In such instances use as few Power Point slides as possible.*

- *If you are using some Power Point slides, glance at them briefly, maintaining as much eye contact as possible with your onlookers. Do not read each word on a slide. Let your audience read the words themselves while you paraphrase the information.*

- *As much as possible, try to memorize your presentation instead of using audiovisual cues. Have a one-page summary close at hand that you can refer to periodically if necessary.*

- *Offer to send audience members a written summary of your presentation if they provide you with their email address. If you do make a Power Point presentation, offer to email your audience a copy of the file. Many speakers object to releasing their slides out of fear that the information will find its way into competitive hands. I do not agree. Spreading your brand and being generous to your audience invariably outweighs the risk of the intellectual property theft of a single presentation.*

MINI STEPS TO SUCCESS

1. Consider Power Point and similar technology more of a detriment than an asset. Employ these tools sparingly.

2. Focus on connecting with your audience through direct talk and constant eye contact.

3. If you must use Power Point, do not read information verbatim from the screen. Paraphrase the material and face your audience, looking at the Power Point slide on a laptop placed between you and the audience, rather than looking at a screen that is behind you. (See Chapter 54.)

———THE TAKEAWAY———

Your number-one priority when speaking before a group is to avoid disconnecting with your audience. Do not jeopardize your connection with them by parroting information in an audiovisual aid or by turning away to read off a screen.

Here's looking at you kid.

—actor Humphrey Bogart in Casablanca

54

IN FULL VIEW: NEVER TURN YOUR BACK ON AN AUDIENCE

I AM NOT A FAN of backs. My own back hurts a lot, especially after 18 holes of golf. I surely do not enjoy looking at them either. When was the last time you looked at someone's back and thought, "Now there is a damn good-looking back"?

You can assume that audience members are equally unenthralled by a speaker's back. In fact, turning one's back to an audience is a common error committed by many speakers who think that dramatically moving around the room will enhance their presentation.

They're wrong. The message is clear: Do not turn your back on your audience.

HERE ARE A FEW SITUATIONS TO AVOID:

- *Walking into an audience. Sure, Johnny Carson and Jay Leno walked into their audience all the time, but that is television. In Speaker World, walking into an audience may sound cool, but every row you walk past represents another row of people who see nothing but your back. Like an invisible electric fence that keeps a dog on property, construct an imaginary barrier between your podium and your audience.*

- *Walking side to side. One of Santa's reindeers was named Prancer, which would be an apt moniker for many misguided speakers. If you absolutely must do wind sprints from side to side in front of your audience, keep your movement to a manageable pace and try to walk with the front of your body facing your audience.*

- *Looking behind you at a screen or some other prop. Turn your neck if you must, but try to keep your body facing the audience.*

- *Speaking in a room with an unusual configuration that compromises your ability to face the entire audience at the same time. In such instances, minimize turning your back by moving carefully and turning around only briefly.*

MINI STEPS TO SUCCESS

1. Rule #1: Never turn your back on an audience or an individual you're speaking with one-on-one. Never. Ever. Rule #2: See Rule #1. (I bet you never heard that little comment before.)

2. Before your talk, scan the room and identify your movement boundaries (e.g., the start of the front row) and potential distractions that may exist behind your podium.

3. If you must turn your back, try to turn only your neck (rather than your entire body) and minimize the time you are traveling in the no-turn lane.

4. Watch other speakers in person, on television, or on social media. When a speaker violates the no-turn rule, assess what caused the violation and what might the speaker have done to avoid it.

———THE TAKEAWAY———

Consciously avoid turning your back to any member of your audience and, when necessary, do it gracefully and for as short a time as possible.

Evaluate one's tone, demeanor and words
and you shall know their character.

—R.J. Intindola, Rising from the Bottom

55

EMBRACE FEEDBACK:
SEEK FORMAL EVALUATIONS

FEW PUBLIC SPEAKERS reach out to their audiences for evaluations of their talks. Granted, the evaluation process is often embedded into event sessions by organizers, so many speakers receive feedback that way, but such feedback tends to be minimal and relatively meaningless.

No matter how seasoned a speaker is, evaluations are still critical. Positive feedback is invariably gratifying and lets a speaker know how well they are doing. Constructive feedback is even more valuable. Even when criticism is unjustified, it can provide the speaker with information on what may have gone stale and a roadmap for how to improve their skills.

Whenever possible, ask your audiences to complete a formal evaluation of your talk. If you have (or can easily get) access to the email addresses of attendees, send everyone an email with a link to an electronic survey. Survey Monkey and other similar platforms are relatively inexpensive and make this process simple and straightforward. If you do not have access to such a list, pass a clipboard around during your talk with a note that says: "I would really value your input regarding my performance today. Please add your name and email address to this list so I can send you a link to a short survey."

Bonus: Every new name and email address can be added

to your master directory for future contact. (See Chapter 56.)

TO DESIGN AN EFFECTIVE
EVALUATION QUESTIONNAIRE:

- *Mix open-ended (written answers) questions with closed-end (scaled or yes/no) ones. Use scaled responses (e.g., "on a scale of ten to one how effective...") as much as possible, rather than "yes/no" questions.*

- *Use open-ended questions to drill down to core issues:*
  "What did you like most about this presentation?"
  "What can the speaker do to improve future presentations?"
  "What was your overall opinion of this presentation?"

- *Use scaled questions to measure how you did on many of the issues addressed in this book, including eye contact, pace, tone, volume, and information flow. A one-to-five scale would do.*

- *Use quantitative data such as scaled scores as tools to measure your progress (or lack thereof) longitudinally. Monitoring trends in your performance (e.g., in what areas are you improving and where are you regressing) is often more important than an overall onetime evaluation score.*

- *Do not react defensively to constructive (or even mean-spirited) criticism. I have dismissed criticism many times only to realize shortly thereafter that it contained more than a grain of truth.*

MINI STEPS TO SUCCESS

1. Do not grow complacent when soliciting evaluations of your performance. Seek an evaluation from your audience as often as possible.

2. Design a master evaluation tool that can be used repeatedly to measure progress over time and that employs many open-ended questions.

3. Engage your audience in the process. Tell them, "I have been doing this a long time and have learned that I can only grow by fully understanding the perspective of my audiences. I value your insight; please help me by completing a short survey."

4. Offer an incentive for audience members to complete the survey—perhaps a raffle for an inexpensive ($25) item or a complimentary 30-minute telephone consultation with you.

5. Swallow your pride. Leave intransigence at the door. Adapting to suggestions is likely to be a win-win proposition for you and your future audiences.

———THE TAKEAWAY———

No one is perfect. We can all benefit from the insight and perspectives of others. Seek out and embrace formal feedback from your audience regarding numerous aspects of your presentation.

*The most important thing in life is the connections
you make with others.*

—fashion designer and filmmaker Tom Ford

56

STAY IN TOUCH: ESTABLISH AN EXPANSIVE CONTACT BASE

I BUILT THE FOUNDATION of my business between 1985 and 1995. After that it grew and flourished until I sold it in 2016. In those early days, new technology appeared in the marketplace virtually every day: fax machines, personal computers, something super-cool called WordPerfect, and car phones. (After I had such a space-eating car phone clunker installed in my 1981 Volvo, no one over 70 pounds could fit in the passenger seat.) What will our techno-wizards think of next?

Social media for one thing.

One professional regret I have is that I was never able to connect with and stay in touch with the thousands of people who attended our conferences or otherwise dealt with me in those pre–social media days. As I launch a postretirement business, I have thousands of LinkedIn contacts and hundreds of Facebook friends to serve as a new foundation. I can only dream of how large those groups would be today if social media existed in 1985.

Moral of the story: Do everything you can to capture a connection to anyone you meet through social media. You never know what the future holds, and you surely want a vehicle for communicating en masse with those who know you.

When you speak before a large group, virtually everyone will know who you are, but you won't know everyone. You want to be able to follow up with as many of these audience members as possible.

YOU HAVE OPTIONS:

1. If a master list of everyone attending your event is available, get a copy. If their email addresses are on the list, send a personalized email to each person saying something about your talk, sharing something of value (e.g., a link to further reading) and including additional links that will help them "friend" you on one or more social media platforms.

2. If you have access to a list, but it contains only names and no email addresses, search your favorite platforms and invite every name on the list to link or friend you.

3. If you do not have access to a master list, pass a clipboard through the audience asking attendees for their name, affiliation, and email address. Offer something in return, such as a complimentary three-month subscription to your Tip of the Week or a free subscription to a periodical.

4. Consider a "leave me your business card" approach. Suggest that audience members leave a business card after your talk so that you can stay in touch and perhaps offer them a complimentary product or service.

MINI STEPS TO SUCCESS

1. Commit to building as large a professional contact list as you can as soon as you can.

2. Determine how you will use your contacts. For example, will you be using social media platforms to share information and grow your business? This decision will likely shape how you build your list.

3. Continue to clean, manage, and expand your list (and the resulting social media contacts).

———THE TAKEAWAY———

Mass communication goes well beyond public speaking. Nothing may be as important to your success as reaching out to vast numbers of people through e-blasts, social media blasts, or the ever-growing opportunities available on YouTube. An information-gathering plan is the essential first step in ensuring that your mass communication efforts reach as many people as possible. Capture connection with anyone you meet on Social Media

VII

NONVERBAL COMMUNICATION

Let's get physical, physical
I want to get physical
Let me hear your body talk, your body talk
Let me hear your body talk
—songwriters Terry Shaddick and
Stephen Alan Kipner, "Let's Get Physical"

57

TURN POSITIVE BODY LANGUAGE HABITS TO YOUR ADVANTAGE

IN 1973 A BOOK titled *Body Language* by Julius Fast was all the rage. Never mind that these days Amazon lists scores of books about body language. In those days Dr. Fast's book was unique and red hot.

I recall having the book with me when I visited a colleague in Nashville, Arkansas. (That's right, Nashville, Arkansas, not Tennessee!) She teased me for reading a "dirty book" (hardly), but it certainly taught me a great deal.

A communicator who can recognize and adapt to common body language cues has a leg up in communication savvy. Some such cues are commonly understood: Folded arms suggest resistance, for example. After a little practice you instinctively begin to interpret a variety of body language gestures, and your reading of them becomes as important to your impact as a communicator as the words themselves.

It goes both ways. The more you learn to recognize

revealing body language in others, the more likely you are to moderate your own body language. Think of body language science as a game of seven-card stud poker. If you can decipher the other person's gestures, you effectively see all their cards—including the three that are face down. Meanwhile the other players can only see your four face-up cards. Play enough hands and become the big winner.

A SAMPLING OF COMMON BODY LANGUAGE CUES INCLUDES:

- *Leaning back (disinterest)*

- *Placing arms across chest (defensiveness, disagreement)*

- *Clasped hands (disinterest)*

- *Touching the nose (disbelief)*

- *Nail-biting (nervousness)*

- *Placing a hand on the cheek (hard at thought)*

- *Tapping or drumming the fingers (impatience)*

- *Tilting a head to one side (intense listening)*

- *Rubbing hands together briskly (anticipation)*

- *Placing the tips of the fingers together (control)*

MINI STEPS TO SUCCESS

1. Create your own inventory of positive and negative body language cues.

2. Incorporate positive body language into your communication style and minimize or eliminate negative body cues.

3. Look for body language cues in other people, whether speaking one-on-one, in group meetings, or giving a presentation. Assess both body language and verbal language in order to genuinely understand the other party.

4. Become a body language decoding zealot. Memorize common body language cues and their likely meaning. Apply your analyses in your personal and professional communications.

———THE TAKEAWAY———

Think of communication as a seven-card stud-poker game. You hear people's words (i.e., the four cards that are turned up), but you can also see their three hole cards—their body language. Learn to interpret the communication of others through a lens that takes in both the verbal and the visual and attempt to assume neutral body language for yourself.

You and that hand jive have got to go,
Willie said "Papa, don't you put me down,
Been doin' that hand jive all over town"
Hand jive, hand jive, hand jive, doin' that crazy hand jive

—*songwriter Johnny Otis, "Willie and the Hand Jive"*

58

ADOPT HAND GESTURES THAT REFLECT WHO YOU ARE

MYTH OR FACT? Those of us of Italian heritage talk with our hands. Although there are surely exceptions to the rule, I think the stereotype holds some truth.

In my humble opinion, what is good for us Italian-Americans is damn well good enough for all of humankind. In moderation, of course, *per favore*.

HAND GESTURES ARE REASONABLE IF THEY:

- *are genuine and not forced*

- *are not so demonstrative as to be distracting*

- *are reasonably relevant to what is being communicated*

- *reflect the "real you"*

- *are made to punctuate an important point*

Many body language experts believe that hand gestures enhance communication and help us make our verbal and mental intentions intelligible to others. Well-timed hand gestures can add structure and emphasis to the spoken word.

According to Carol Kinsey Goman, noted author and educator, "Gesture is really linked to speech, and gesturing while you talk can really power up your thinking. Gesturing can help people form clearer thoughts, speak in tighter sentences and use more declarative language."

MINI STEPS TO SUCCESS

1. Accept that hand gestures can be an invaluable tool for effective communicators if the gestures are not forced or overwhelming.

2. Experiment and discover when hand gestures work well for you. Do such gestures help you structure your communication? Do they help you make a salient point? Are hand gestures useful when you are enumerating some type of numerical list?

3. Take videos of yourself speaking with others. Observe your hands. Are they overactive? If so, when did you use hand gestures, and how relevant were they to what you were saying at the time? Are your hand gestures too static? How can you use your hands in a different manner?

When hand gestures are legitimate, relevant, and not forced, they can help structure and punctuate your communication. Hand gestures should not be over the top, but do not eliminate them either. Be yourself.

Question: "What do you give a 500-pound gorilla with diarrhea?"
Answer: "plenty of room."

—*My father-in-law, Ray Manini's, favorite joke*

59

GIVE THEM ROOM: BE CONSIDERATE OF PERSONAL SPACE

I HAVE SEEN IT ALL. People who stand so close I feel claustrophobic and threatened. People who create so much room I'm compelled to immediately pop a breath mint. In both instances, the conversation is likely to be uncomfortable.

Here are some useful rules for gauging the right amount of personal space in a one-on-one conversation:

Be conscious of what you feel is a proper distance between yourself and the other party. Know the boundaries of your personal comfort zone.

Observe the other party's reaction to your spacing. Do they appear uncomfortable by your physical presence? Do they tend to tilt their body back? Perhaps that's a signal for you to retreat a step or two. Do they seem to be edging a bit toward you? You may be standing too far away.

Strive for a compromise. Blend your "keep-my-distance comfort zone" with what you perceive to be their comfort zone.

Do not be a rigid mannequin. (See Chapter 41.) Move

a little, shift left to right, but keep your movements subtle. (Do not break into a peppy rendition of the cha-cha-cha.)

The same rules apply whether both parties are standing or sitting. Learn to be aware of your comfort zone when you're sitting down.

Be considerate of the way personal space extends beyond body positioning. Psychological spacing, particularly with business associates and loved ones, is also a vital form of communication. Regardless of your personality type, try not to overwhelm anyone with attention, either positive or negative. Do not be shy about asking someone if they need more physical space. Many people are reluctant to offer this information on their own yet are invariably appreciative of someone else showing such consideration.

MINI STEPS TO SUCCESS

1. Begin to observe how others space themselves in one-on-one conversations. Let them take the lead and see what happens. You will likely learn a lot about traditional comfort zones.

2. Equipped with this knowledge, develop your own sense of distance.

3. Observe how others react to your need for space. Quickly adjust your position in line with their perceived needs.

4. Include small but appropriate movement during your interactions.

5. Factor inquiries about space into your conversation

and be forthright about asking others if they need more space.

—————THE TAKEAWAY—————
Improper spacing can torpedo otherwise promising communication. Plan and execute your physical and psychological spacing carefully.

The things you say, the things you don't say, the things you do,
or the things you don't do are always sending a loud
message to those around you.
What kind of a message are you sending?
Is it a true reflection of who you are?"
—*Lindsey Rietzsch,* Successful Failures: Recognizing the Divine Role
That Opposition Plays in Life's Quest for Success

60

YOU CAN MISREAD:
PROBE NONVERBAL SIGNALS

ON MORE THAN one occasion I have responded with a visual snarl to an innocuous question posed by my wife of 40-plus years. My snarl often had nothing to do with her comment. I may have barely heard her words but rather was thinking of some other irritant at that moment. (e.g., "Darn, the Mets' bullpen blew another game last night!") After that, my usually ultra-perceptive wife might misread my facial expression and quickly jump on a false narrative.

It happens all the time. Unless you are a master mind reader—a rare trait these days—chances are that you, too, from time to time will misread another person's nonverbal signals.

There is only one viable "get out of jail free" card. You need to probe at the first sign of potentially ambiguous displeasure. What if the ever-perceptive Ms. L. said to me, "You look concerned. If so, please elaborate?"

TWO THINGS ARE LIKELY TO COME OUT OF THIS:

- *I will respond that I am in fact concerned and will say why, thus potentially diffusing the issue, or...*

- *I will respond that I am not concerned at all and was thinking about something else ("those darn relief pitchers!"), thus diffusing the issue. Either way it's a win-win. (Unless we deny our real concern, but who among us would ever do that?)*

MINI STEPS TO SUCCESS

1. Accept the notion that your interpretation of someone's body language may be incorrect.

2. Calmly probe to determine if your interpretation has merit.

3. Observe the other party's body language when they respond to your questions. Are you comfortable with their denial?

4. If the other party does exhibit concern, consider that admission to be valuable information: You have identified a problem that, if left unchecked, may fester and run counter to your communication goal.

———THE TAKEAWAY———

Things are not always what they appear to be. Nonverbal cues can be more important than verbal ones, but they must be interpreted properly. Learn to probe for legitimacy at the first sign of negative nonverbal communication. Misinterpretations have foiled many a good plan.

*In an age of constant movement, nothing
is more urgent than sitting still.*

—*travel writer and essayist Pico Iyer*

61

MAKE YOURSELF AT HOME:
SIT WHEN NECESSARY

REMEMBER MY excruciatingly long day in Detroit when I had to speak for six hours on nada sleep? (See Chapter 38.) Imagine speaking before 40 people all day after pulling an all-nighter. Misery.

What you likely do not know is that I delivered part of my presentation from a chair. I was a little tired at some point, so I sat down briefly. Later, I thought, boy, I can't go on much longer, and sat down again. And when I could tell from the body language of my audience that I was beginning to lose them, yup, I sat down one more time.

You do not need to be standing in order to wow an audience. Far more important is that you feel comfortable and give your best presentation, whether you are standing, sitting, or lying down. (Please reserve option number three for extreme emergencies.) I have often used a chair as a prop when speaking before a small group or giving a public presentation.

*HERE ARE SOME POINTERS FROM SITTING
BULL, YOUR FRIENDLY AUTHOR:*

- *Accept the notion that audiences or small groups generally do not mind if you address them while seated.*

- *Always have a chair handy, whether you plan to use it or not.*

- *Consider that there are many reasons that justify a brief sitting period. You may be tired, nursing an injury, or feel that alternating positions would better keep your audience alert.*

- *Use a high stool, if available. A high stool is usually better than a normal chair, since it provides you with a clearer sightline and may afford the audience a better view of you.*

- *Maintain the same speaking style when you are seated as when standing—using hand gestures, body movements, speed, pace, and tone.*

Neither a large audience nor a small group is likely to notice or care if you alternate between sitting and standing during a presentation. They are more likely to be focused on what you are saying and how you are saying it.

MINI STEPS TO SUCCESS

1. Do not be afraid of sitting during a presentation. Embrace it.

2. Order a stool or chair for every one of your presentations. Keep the chair within arm's reach. You may not use it, but a chair can be as essential to your talk as a microphone.

3. Do not call attention to the fact that you are sitting

down. (Avoid saying, "Excuse me a moment, my back hurts and I need to sit.")

4. Seamlessly and quietly transition between sitting and standing positions.

5. Whether standing or sitting, continue to focus on the principles of effective speaking.

———THE TAKEAWAY———

The value of changing pace applies to more than just the oral aspect of your presentation. You can also change pace by alternating between sitting and standing. Sitting is also an excellent way to temporarily rest and re-energize your body without detracting from your presentation.

And she'll have fun, fun, fun
'Til her daddy takes the T-bird away
(Fun, fun, fun 'til her daddy takes the T-bird away)

—Beach Boys Michael Love and Brian Wilson, "Fun, Fun, Fun"

62

CHILL OUT:
HAVE SOME FUN

POP QUIZ: Who are the three most fun people you know? Go ahead, name names. Why do you think these people are fun? Who are the three least fun people that you know? Why are they not fun? Finally, which of these two triumvirates would you think are better communicators?

The odds are stacked in favor of the fun group. Having conducted training sessions on sales and communication for decades, I discovered that blending a fun personality with a fun environment tends to make people more engaged and eager to learn.

To qualify as a fun person, you don't have to crack jokes all the time. But you do need a lighthearted sensibility and a creative spirit that comes through in the way you communicate.

The flavor of this book serves as Exhibit A. Do readers prefer a style that blends humor, anecdotes, and real-life experiences to reinforce my basic messages? Or would they appreciate a more serious, philosophical approach that reads like a textbook? I'll let you make that choice.

The bottom line is: Do not shy away from injecting a

large dose of fun into your approach to communication. When people are put at ease through laughter and conviviality, they are more likely to remain engaged and favorably responsive to your messages. Few of us are comfortable with rigid, overly serious, "the world is about to end" personalities.

MINI STEPS TO SUCCESS

1. Recognize that having fun does not necessarily mean saying funny things. Rather, embed something light into your communication, provided such diversion is consistent with the overall mood of the occasion.

2. Fun, in the context of communication with others, often involves innovative questions, minigames, and audience interaction with the speaker or fellow audience members.

3. Judge the mood of your audiences, both before a presentation and during your talk, in order to assess the degree to which a fun approach may be appropriate. Scale down or back off your fun mode when it does not seem right for the moment.

4. In the immortal words of *Mad* magazine's Alfred E. Neuman, "What—Me Worry?" Few things are matters of life and death. Relax, enjoy yourself, have fun, and stop worrying.

Both oral and written communication, whether before a group or one-on-one, tend to be effective when a little bit of levity is part of your approach. Smile, laugh, relax, and introduce an element of fun into your interactions.

VIII

EMAIL
COMMUNICATION

How to write a good email:
1. Write your email 2. Delete most of it 3. Send

—Daniel Munz, Senior Advisor, U.S. Department of State

63

DEVELOP A ROUTINE
EMAIL STRUCTURE

I AM RETIRED from the nine-to-five world these days, doing little more than writing this book and hanging out. Yet at this moment, 56,474 emails are stored in my computer's sent folder. And that does not include tens of thousands of previously deleted sent emails that I deemed unworthy of keeping. Think that emails are an important part of my communication life?

If sending emails is central to your professional or personal life, be vigilant about how you construct them. Virtually all the tips on written communication in previous chapters (brevity, structure, highlighting key phrases, to name a few) apply to emails, along with a few extras.

WHEN YOU WRITE AN EMAIL, TRY TO:

- *Follow Dan Munz's advice: Blast out a draft, delete whatever you can, reread the draft again, clean the draft a little more, and only then hit the send button.*

- *Put thought into your subject line. (See Chapter 68.) Be highly selective when you use the blind carbon copy (bcc) function. (See Chapter 64.)*

- *State the objective of the email at the outset (e.g., "I am writing today in order to…").*

- *Summarize the keys points of the email at the end (e.g., "In summary…).*

- *Make most emails visually striking by using bullets, different font sizes, colors, shading, and the box function. Be an email artist but be aware that not all computers display these formats in the same way.*

- *Maintain an inventory of more than one signature line for different types of emails, (e.g., personal vs. professional). Be thoughtful about what you include, such as a website link, your mobile and other relevant phone numbers, and/or a favorite quote.*

- *Recognize that an email can be easily shared and thus fall into the wrong hands. Whether the email is confidential or not, never write something that may be harmful to you if viewed by the wrong eyes.*

MINI STEPS TO SUCCESS

1. If available, determine the number of both incoming and outgoing emails that you received and sent during the past year. The number of emails in each of these folders will likely surprise you.

2. Write a first draft of every email and delete as much extraneous information as necessary. (See Chapter 23.) Chop, chop, chop.

3. Write most emails using the same structure and flow as a public presentation: overview-core-summary.

4. Create a series of alternative signature lines, including related links, and select appropriate options for different emails (e.g., personal vs. professional).

──────THE TAKEAWAY──────

Develop a routine for constructing outgoing emails. Outgoing emails are the heart of your professional and personal life. Make every email relevant, to the point, and easy to read. Then make them even more relevant, to the point, and easy to read.

For your eyes only, can see me through the night
For your eyes only, I never need to hide.
You can see so much in me, so much in me that's new
I never felt until I looked at you
—songwriters Bill Conti and Michael Leeson, "For Your Eyes Only"

64

ENSURE TRANSPARENCY: USE CC AND BCC WISELY

ONCE UPON A TIME I used the blind carbon copy (bcc) function of an email extensively. What a great way to keep others in the loop without anyone else knowing about it! Or so I thought. Then, oops. Big-time change of heart.

Somewhere along the line it dawned on me that the practice bordered on the unscrupulous. If I am on the receiving end of an email and later learn that others received a blind carbon copy, I would probably not be happy.

Care must also be taken to ensure that you manage the carbon copy (cc) distribution of your emails as well. On the surface, naming every cc recipient provides transparency and can only help to keep multiple parties on the same page. And, indeed, that is often true. On the other hand, the cc function can be overused and provide too much and often irrelevant information to too many people. To say nothing of filling in-boxes with unnecessary and unwelcome clutter. Spend time considering exactly who should see each email you write, before you hit the send button.

SOME CC/BCC RULES:

- *Do not be a cc zealot just for the sake of transparency. Use the function only when parties other than the primary recipients of your email legitimately need to see your email.*

- *Use the bcc function rarely, if at all. Ask yourself why a candidate for a blind carbon copy cannot be included in the carbon copy line. There are occasions when it is appropriate for a person to receive a blind carbon copy, but short of an emergency, such times are rare.*

- *Do use the bcc function when you are sending an email blast to a large group (e.g., 10 or more) or a smaller group that should not be privy to the email addresses of some or all the other names on the list. On many occasions I have received such a list in the cc column and noticed email addresses of high-profile individuals who would not want their contact information made public. When you do send out such blasts, put your email address in the "to" line and bcc your distribution list.*

MINI STEPS TO SUCCESS

1. Do not take your cc and bcc email distribution functions for granted. A mistake can have significant consequences.

2. Review your cc and bcc lists one last time before hitting the send button.

3. Recognize that the bcc function can be your friend if you use it primarily to protect the confidentially of other people's email addresses.

——THE TAKEAWAY——

The cc and bcc functions of your email distribution strategy can have powerful implications, both pro and con. Review the appropriate use of these functions prior to sending any email.

Pretty woman, stop awhile
Pretty woman, talk awhile
Pretty woman, give your smile to me
—*songwriters Bill Dees and Roy Orbison, "Oh, Pretty Woman"*

65

PRETTY PLEASE: MAKE YOUR EMAILS VISUALLY ATTRACTIVE

HAVE YOU NOTICED that people read less nowadays? Far less. Our society appears to have settled into an information era centered around headline news, short *USA Today* features, social-media blurbs, YouTube video training, and mini "how to" books. Reading a traditional newspaper, watching an hour-long newscast, and writing long letters are just so 20th century.

Shortly after I conceptualized this book, I realized that a tome with extensive paragraphs, one after another, on the intricacies and theoretical underpinnings of good communication, would bore readers to the nth degree. Better to offer 77 short chapters, characterized by key points and takeaways, to keep readers engaged and learning.

Govern construction of your emails with the same easy-to-read spirit. At a minimum, ensure that your outgoing emails are as brief and direct as possible by relying on short sentences and bullet points.

SPIFFING UP YOUR EMAILS
SHOULD HAVE TWO PHASES:

- *Phase I: Keep your sentences and paragraphs as short as possible. Consider using even super short (e.g., one- or two-sentence) paragraphs, even if such a structure is contrary to conventional practices. After all, you are not vying for a Nobel Prize in literature just yet. You are merely striving to get your point across.*

- *Phase II: Use the broad array of graphic tools available in most word-processing systems to make your message as attractive and easy to absorb as possible.*

All email recipients are not cut from the same cloth, nor are various emails, which may range from lighthearted correspondence with friends to serious business matters. Your appropriate degree of "decoration" will vary accordingly.

MINI STEPS TO SUCCESS

1. Draft every email with the intention of making your wording concise, attractive, and easy to read.

2. Proof all your outgoing emails and ask yourself if the recipients will find the email attractive and easy to read.

3. Develop a clear email style that suits your personality. Add color, use checks or bullet points, make lists, and so on as appropriate.

4. Alter your artistic input to suit both the nature and the tone of your message.

————THE TAKEAWAY————

Prior to hitting the send button on an outgoing email, ask yourself if the email is easy to read. If the answer is no, make the email shorter, better spaced, and more attractive.

Some things that happen for the first time
Seem to be happening again
And so it seems that we have met before
And laughed before, and loved before
But who knows where or when?

—*lyricist Richard Rodgers, "Where or When"*

66

FILE/FILE/FILE: DEVELOP AN EASILY ACCESSIBLE EMAIL ARCHIVAL SYSTEM

DESPITE PERIODIC purges, I currently retain more than 100,000 emails in my received and sent email boxes. Little wonder it takes me mega-minutes to find an old email, if I find it at all. And I am a card-carrying member of Hyper-organized Anonymous, no less. Heaven help the chronically disorganized Average Albert.

Step one in developing an easily accessible email archival system is to archive as few emails as possible. Ask yourself if you really, really, really must keep a given message that you have sent or received. Be hard on yourself. Take pride in how few emails you have saved, not how massive your archive of ancient messages.

Step two is to purge your current email files, big time. I prefer to first sort my sent file by "to" and my received files by "from" and then purge entire clusters of senders/recipients from both groups. Extraneous emails disappear by the thousands. To coin a phrase: "chop, chop, chop."

Step three is to create numerous folders and subfolders within your system. For example, I use separate mega-folders for my personal and professional emails. Within each of these mega-folders I keep numerous subfolders and, in some instances, subfolders for the subfolders. And then I list them in alphabetical order.

Finally, I repeat the purge process at least once a year. Despite my noble intentions, numerous irrelevant emails find their way into my archives between purges. Pare down your email fat at periodic intervals.

MINI STEPS TO SUCCESS

1. Time is one of your most important assets. A clean email archival system is a time saver and will encourage you to cross-check old correspondence without losing too much time (or not finding that critical email at all).

2. Develop a system to manage both your received and sent emails from the outset. Set up folders and subfolders and list them alphabetically. If you already have large sent and received email folders, sort them by recipient or sender, purge extraneous emails, and then move each recipient or sender to their proper subfolder.

3. Purging emails is a never-ending process. Schedule a purge day at least once a year.

———THE TAKEAWAY———

Develop a detailed email archival system and stick with it. Differentiate between "must keep" emails and those that are unlikely to be of value. Take advantage of subfile options available on most systems.

You can lead a horse to water,
but you can't make him drink.
—12th-century English proverb
(favored by my RAND Corporation mentor, Dr. Steve Klein)

67

INCLUDE LINKS
AND ATTACHMENTS

IN THE PROCESS of researching this book, I read an article that suggested one should never add an attachment to or use a link in an outgoing email. Au contraire, sweet readers, au contraire. Granted, some users fear opening attachments because of malware concerns, but in most circumstances using attachments is accepted.

Links and attachments are frequently a core element of the communicator's tool kit. The electronic versions of newspapers, ranging from the *New York Times* to your local rag, use links to provide readers an easy connection to in-depth information. Blogs, online-information portals, and social media use such links widely as well. Why not emails?

HERE ARE SOME SUGGESTIONS:

- *Maintain an inventory of your favorite links and potential attachments. For example, add useful websites to your favorites list so the links can be easily located, copied, and pasted into an outgoing message. Likewise, develop a file of favorite attachments, such as emotional stories and subject overviews.*

- *Seek opportunities to send links and include attachments. Professional emails can be spruced up by sending a link or attachment on a professional topic of mutual interest to the recipient. For example, if a colleague is interested in becoming a great communicator, send them a link to a website where they can order this book!*

- *Consider fun links and attachments as well. I maintain an inventory of about 5,000 photos, mostly of friends, both new and old, on both my personal computer and devices and often attach a memorable photo when emailing with old friends.*

- *If you mention an organization in your email, consider adding a link to its website (e.g., "Try the Rocky Mountainair train from Vancouver to Banff (https://www.rockymountaineer.com/routes_destinations)."*

MINI STEPS TO SUCCESS

1. Recognize that adding a link to an outgoing email or including an attachment adds value without making the body of the email longer. But be aware that some recipients are leery of opening an attachment from a sender they do not recognize.

2. Create an electronic attachment and link library of your favorite links and most frequently distributed attachments.

3. Include fun items as well as serious professional items in your inventory. Photos and humorous stories are two examples of lighter links or attachments.

4. Google any topic or organization that may be relevant to an aspect of your email and include a link to that website in your email. Finding and moving a website address to your email takes seconds but often comes across as thoughtful, helpful, and professional.

————THE TAKEAWAY————

Well-conceived attachments and links to websites are a means to say more with less. The body of your email can remain concise, while the recipient receives an option to learn more. Doing the work for them enhances your credibility and makes life easier for those on the receiving end of your email.

What's it all about, Alfie?
Is it just for the moment we live?
What's it all about when you sort it out, Alfie?
Are we meant to take more than we give

—songwriters Burt Bacharach and Hal David, "Alfie"

68

WHAT'S IT ALL ABOUT? CHOOSE YOUR SUBJECT LINE CAREFULLY

DURING THE PAST YEAR I have noticed that my email spam filter has been working well. More than 100 unwanted emails find their way into my spam folder every day. Yet numerous unwanted emails continue to sneak into my primary in-box.

I seldom read an email from anyone I do not know. I even ignore some from people I do know who fail the readability test. What drives my decision to not open an email message?

It's largely about the subject line. List a subject that piques my interest, and I may look further. Offer the same old tired platitude, and I cannot hit my delete button fast enough. A sender needs to fashion a subject line that could arouse sufficient interest from the recipient to open the email.

SOME SUGGESTIONS FOR MAKING YOUR SUBJECT LINE MORE APPEALING INCLUDE:

- *Make the subject line about something of value for the recipient. Remember WIIFM (what's in it for me). (See Chapter 18.)*

- *Avoid tired language. Leave the "last chance to..." phrase to the guy at the used-car dealership.*

- *If the email is personal rather than professional, give the subject line individual flair.*

- *Avoid exclamation points and other dramatic punctuation.*

- *Connect the topic on the subject line with the first line of your email.*

MINI STEPS TO SUCCESS

1. Do not take the subject line of an outgoing email for granted. The appeal of the subject line is often the deciding factor in whether a recipient will open the message.

2. Establish a series of rules regarding your subject lines. Such rules may include use of trite language, abbreviations, certain punctuations, and tired appeals.

3. Notice keywords or phrases in emails from unknown senders that arouse your interest. Mentally inventory these keywords for future use in your email subject lines.

There is a thin line between the decision to open an email or to discard it. The subject line is often the key factor. Your subject line must stimulate interest and trust by persuading the recipient the email offers him value.

You say yes, I say no
You say stop and I say go, go, go, oh no
—*Beatles John Lennon and Paul McCartney, "Hello, Goodbye"*

69

BACK TO YOU:
COPY KEY POINTS WHEN
RESPONDING TO AN EMAIL

ACCURACY is central to effective communication. In both conversation and written correspondence, it is easy to misquote or misinterpret another person's comments or questions, thus creating a downward communication spiral.

CONSIDER FOLLOWING THIS SEQUENCE:

- *Copy/paste key comments or questions from an incoming email into outgoing emails that involve a response to your sender. Copy and paste the entire incoming email or extract only specific comments or questions that require a response.*

- *Do not discriminate between professional and personal emails. I apply this principal to both audiences.*

- *Separate each comment or question and its corresponding response by at least one blank line. Your response will look like it is in a question/answer format, as opposed to a unilateral response.*

- *Clearly separate the incoming question/comment from your response. For example, I often show the question in black and my response in a different color. Or place a question in regular type and your response in bold. Or try matching questions in regular type with their corresponding answers in italics. You get the idea.*

The question/answer format provides numerous benefits: It permits you to match your answer specifically to the exact question or point. It also provides a greater sense of focus on the question or comment at hand. It reminds the other party of their exact words, minimizes misinterpretations and misunderstandings, and creates a format for a subsequent ongoing dialogue.

MINI STEPS TO SUCCESS

1. Recognize that the copy/paste method of responding to an email appears professional, tends to minimize misunderstandings, and adds resonance to your response.

2. Develop your own cut/paste style. Focus on certain portions of incoming emails or establish a color-coded or otherwise contrasting visual style in your response.

3. Think in terms of constructing your response in a question/answer format rather than in the usual narrative one.

─────THE TAKEAWAY─────

It is easy to extract a question or key point from an incoming email, paste the question or point in your responding message, and then append your response to that question or point. Such a practice provides a more direct response and lessens the potential for misinterpretations.

Un dat un dat un dat dat, un dat un dat, dat dat
Un dat un dat un dat dat, un dat un dat dat
—*songwriter Melvin Schwartz, "Baby Talk"*

70
LOL IMHO: MINIMIZE ABBREVIATIONS AND ACRONYMS

THERE ARE EXCEPTIONS, but in general I prefer to avoid abbreviations, commonly used acronyms, and popular social media–orientated acronyms. Most exceptions pertain to personal email correspondence with people I know well. When communicating with friends, there are times when a well-placed OMG or LOL makes perfect sense.

OTOH ("on the other hand," for the uninitiated), I prefer going old school and consciously omit slang, abbreviations, and acronyms when messaging anyone who is not a friend or family member. The recipient may not be able to decipher the acronym or may find it slick or flippant.

During the dying days of snail mail (the 1990s), I asked my staff to update our company's mailing list of about 14,000 names and addresses by completing a series of search-and-replace activities on our mailing database. Common address abbreviations such as Rd., Ave., and Blvd. became "Road," "Avenue," and "Boulevard," respectively. C.E.O. became "Chief Executive Officer" and "Nor." became "North."

Why so much time and toil devoted to a seemingly minor change? Because the refined addresses looked a tad cleaner and more professional, and my goal was to persuade every recipient of our print mail to open the envelope or brochure and explore its contents.

Updating an individual address may not add up to anything, but 14,000 cleaner-looking addresses gave the company a more professional look. The same principle of no-nonsense professionalism applies to your email practices.

You may have only one chance to make a favorable impression on recipients of your email. Why not present yourself in a highly professional manner?

MINI STEPS TO SUCCESS

1. Be selective in deciding when to use abbreviations and acronyms.

2. Modern-day social media–oriented acronyms can be clever and fun, but you need to ensure that your audience is hip enough to know the meaning of each one.

3. Consider how unknown a given acronym may be before using it. If there is a likelihood that a reader won't be familiar with it, parenthetically define the acronym. e.g., "Koehn's ERA (earned-run average) is now only 1.65."

4. In most instances, avoid abbreviations altogether. A spelled-out word looks better than its abbreviation and is less likely to be misinterpreted.

————THE TAKEAWAY————

Be discreet whenever you use abbreviations and acronyms, particularly in your professional correspondence. When in doubt, always travel the more formal road. This rule can usually be tempered when you are dealing with personal friends and acquaintances.

IX

OTHER FORMS
OF COMMUNICATION

If you build it, he will come.
—Mysterious voice speaking to actor Kevin Costner
in Field of Dreams

71

BE PROACTIVE: DEVELOP A SOCIAL MEDIA PLAN

WHEN IT COMES to effective mass communication, some of our nation's highest-profile communicators achieved their status by mastering the latest technologies.

Political success is a prime example of people using the latest technology to their advantage. Franklin D. Roosevelt mastered the use of radio through his fireside chats. John F. Kennedy and, later, Ronald Reagan, mastered television as a communications medium with their innate charisma and acting ability, respectively. One could argue that Donald Trump mastered the art of using his Twitter feed to reach his core constituency.

It stands to reason that as great communicators emerge in the future, they will succeed in part by mastering the emerging communications tools of their day.

Social media is now at the epicenter of the mass communication landscape. The use of social media, in some way, is going to be central to expanding the effectiveness of your communications.

HERE ARE A FEW SUGGESTIONS
TO GET GOING:

- *Learn what every popular social media platform offers, the type of audience that each platform reaches, and how it lets users reach out to masses of individuals. You can't manage the team if you don't know its players.*

- *Maintain at least a minimal presence on multiple social media platforms. Learn how to use each platform so you have a foundation if you wish to use that platform more actively.*

- *Develop a social media style consistent with your personality, lifestyle, and skill set. Do you have a commanding presence? Start a YouTube channel. Are you doing interesting things? Let the world know via Facebook. Do you love to take photos? Welcome to Instagram.*

- *Develop a short term/long term social media plan consistent with your personal and professional aspirations and skills.*

MINI STEPS TO SUCCESS

1. Be active in social media in a way that will establish a strong presence and hone your skills for more active engagement later.

2. Be flexible and selective. There are many social media platforms and a broad continuum of involvement levels, from highly passive to exceptionally engaged.

3. Keep an eye on social media trends to determine

which platforms are gaining in demographic reach and which are fading.

———THE TAKEAWAY———

Social media is rapidly becoming central to communications on multiple levels worldwide. The relevance of the platforms is unlikely to abate for decades to come. Be certain that your ability to connect with others through social media is part of your long-term communications plan.

No struggle, no success. The strongest thunder strikes often bring the heaviest rainfall. The weight of your fulfillment depends on how wide you cast your nets.

—Isrealmore Ayivor, The Daily Drive 365

72

CAST A WIDE NET: MAINTAIN A BROAD PRESENCE

M ANY DECADES AGO, I needed a date to accompany me to a special event. I asked one nice lady after another after another and yet another and received a corsage of four "no thank yous." The fifth time was a charm. I showed up at the event with a lovely lady on my arm, and only I knew of my abysmal .200 get-a-date batting average.

Life is a numbers game. Get twice as many at bats and you will likely get twice as many home runs. Tim Anderson of the Chicago White Sox was the major league's leading hitter in 2019 with a solid .335 batting average. Guess what: Tim failed to get a hit in 66.5 percent of his official at bats. Failure is never failure if you show up at the metaphorical home plate enough times.

Communicate to more people more frequently. If you are communicating a message to a large group, find a way to make that group even larger.

HOW CAN YOU DO THAT?

- *Continually focus on building your contact base, whether it's by expanding your mailing list or by widening your social media reach.*

- *Post more often on social media. A wide net is one thing. Reinforcing your message is another.*

- *Encourage recipients of your written communications to forward certain emails and text messages, to retweet your tweets, or to resend your posts.*

- *Have multiple contact points for each person on your list. When possible, try to establish social media links and maintain current email addresses, business and/or residential addresses, and telephone numbers. If you rely on only a single contact point for each person and that person's contact changes (e.g., they are no longer on Facebook or have a new email address), you may have lost them forever. Best to have multiple contact points.*

MINI STEPS TO SUCCESS

1. Recognize that strong mass communication involves expanding your base and repeating your message. Modern telecommunication tools facilitate this process.

2. Set loose quotas. Resolve to add some number of new contacts to your base every day. Five new contacts a day equals 1,825 new contacts a year (or 1,830 every leap year)! Similarly, set a goal for the number of social media posts you write per week. But do not overdo it; few of us like social media posting pests.

3. Learn to craft messages (both traditional and for social media) in a manner that overtly or subtly encourages recipients to forward your message to others.

———THE TAKEAWAY———

Mass communication is a numbers game. Optimal effectiveness involves expanding your outreach to more individuals, encouraging others to forward your message, and sharing your message more often.

A person must live in harmony with his or her inner self while recognizing a vital connection to the entire world.

—*Kilroy J. Oldster,* Dead Toad Scrolls

73

HAVE A HEART: BE EMPATHETIC

APPROACH EVERY communication with a flexible, open mind. Try to listen to and understand the other person's point of view, as opposed to single-mindedly pursuing your own message. By entering a more sensitive dialogue, even with people whom you may disagree with, you will enjoy more honest and productive conversations.

In many communications your primary goal is to achieve your objective. At times a focus on your objective alone will result in a tunnel-vision sense of purpose. Your focus and energy will reflect your needs—what you hope to get out of the communication. The strong communicator will instinctively size up the other party's vulnerabilities, either through their words or body language.

ONCE YOU HAVE NOTICED SOME UNEASINESS IN ANOTHER PARTY, YOU CAN MOVE IN THESE DIRECTIONS:

- *Clarify the issue. The problem may be directly related to the subject at hand. Or the other party may be uneasy about dealing with you. Or the concern may have nothing to do with you or the topic of discussion. Sort this out right away.*

- *Muster a modicum of genuine empathy. If empathy is not your strong suit, try as best you can with phrases such as "I understand…" or "I'm terribly sorry that…."*

- *Do not take every issue personally. Everybody has bad days or bad moments within an otherwise good day, or they may be dealing with a personal matter that you simply do not know or understand.*

- *Generating empathy does not always come naturally. What seems minor or trivial to you may be troubling to the other party. Give the other party the benefit of the doubt.*

MINI STEPS TO SUCCESS

1. Assess the other party's sense of spirit. Their spirit may be expressed through their words, how they articulate those words, their facial expression, or their body language.

2. Recognize that any concerns they express may not have anything to do with you or the issue under discussion.

3. Continually place yourself in the other party's shoes. If they appear to be troubled by something, take them at their word and be empathetic.

Otherwise flawless communication can easily unravel if the other party has a concern and you fail to recognize and acknowledge that issue. The concern may have nothing to do with you or the subject under discussion. A great communicator needs to be sensitive and effectively communicate this sensitivity to others.

Not so fast, Louis. Nobody is going to be arrested.
Not for a while yet.
—actor Humphrey Bogart to Claude Rains in Casablanca

74

SPICK-AND-SPAN:
CLEAN YOUR IN-BOX

TIMELY RESPONSES are central to effective email and other communication (e.g., a voice or text mail message). You can be a "lights out" communicator, but the recipient of your communication may well turn the lights out on you if you fiddle and diddle too much before responding to their message.

Being a poster child for my fellow Virgos (i.e., the hyper-organized birth sign), I try to look at a piece of paper only upon receipt and process or file it away immediately. The same policy applies to my email in-box.

I am typing these words at 7:04 a.m. During the past 30 minutes, I processed about 20 emails that appeared in my in-box overnight. My in-box is now empty. I am happy! Message: Clean your in-box as soon as you are exposed to incoming email.

WHAT'S THE RATIONALE?

- *Your near-immediate response is invariably appreciated by senders.*

- *An issue is often raised in an email that is time sensitive, and an immediate response is necessary.*

317

- *An empty in-box means that an important incoming email is less likely to be accidently overlooked and thereby ignored.*

One more point, learned the hard way. Sort your incoming email by "from" so that multiple emails from the same sender can be batched. Read every new email from that sender before you respond to any of their emails. I used to respond to the oldest "new" email first only to learn that additional information surfaced on emails sent a short time later. Keep the bigger picture in mind.

Okay. You have my permission: Stop reading this book for a few minutes, go directly to your email in-box, and clean it up. Trust me, you will feel much better!

MINI STEPS TO SUCCESS

1. Commit to processing every email as quickly as possible.

2. Begin each morning by processing every email that arrived since you last checked your in-box.

3. Continue to process every incoming email you receive during the day in as close to real time as possible.

4. Apply the same rapid-response policy to other forms of communication, such as voice mail messages, text messages, and old-fashioned snail mail.

———THE TAKEAWAY———

Become a zealous email early responder. Develop a system whereby you constantly strive to keep your in-box empty. Such a policy will enhance the effectiveness of your communication, generate greater respect from your email partners, and make life simpler for you.

You catch more flies with honey than you do with vinegar.
—old proverb

75

RETREAT: HANDLING A DIFFICULT COMMUNICATION

I DO NOT REMEMBER exactly when. Or where. Or why. But I do remember being rude and irrational toward a fellow motorist over a mere parking spot many years ago. I doubt my anger at his perceived transgression had any merit. Imagine my surprise when Mr. Fellow Motorist responded in a calm, kind, and rationale manner. However, he did more that day than calm me down. He provided a role model for me and everyone else by staying above the fray when faced with a threatening, if irrational, provocation.

Even the greatest communicator may falter and initiate a verbal (or written) confrontation or respond in kind to a provocation. Don't succumb. Whether you feel that you are in the right or not, head directly to rationality mode whenever you sense trouble.

TO DEFUSE CONFRONTATIONS:

- *Assume that any stranger is inherently a good, decent person unless and until proven otherwise.*

- *No matter how wrong the other party may seem to be, always give them the benefit of the doubt.*

- *Turn around and walk away from a potential conflict whenever possible.*

- *Keep the metaphorical honey readily available while leaving your vinegar at the door. That is, always take the high road.*

- *Alleviate another person's concern by apologizing first, even if you are 101 percent certain you are in the right.*

- *Ask the other party if there is anything you can do to make things right.*

- *Never express anger in writing. (See Chapter 25.)*

- *Avoid negative body language and ill-chosen words. Tame those flailing arms and angry looks.*

MINI STEPS TO SUCCESS

1. As my mother-in-law, Terry Mainini, often said, resolve to "always be the bigger person."

2. Develop a diversion strategy for angry communications that you might initiate as well as confrontations sparked by someone else.

3. Expressing anger goes beyond words. Keep an eye on inappropriate body language.

———THE TAKEAWAY———

Confrontation—whether verbal, written, or through body language—is typically counterproductive. Learn to soothe, rather than exacerbate, tensions by remaining calm, fair, and rational.

You lie!
—Representative Joe Wilson (R-SC), heckling President Barack Obama's
2009 State of the Union address

76

BIG LITTLE LIES.
ALWAYS TELL THE TRUTH

HERE'S A NOVEL IDEA: Always tell the truth. Such advice goes without saying when you are talking about outright fabrication. If you happen to be a pathological liar, you should probably be reading a few other books rather than this one. What I am talking about here are nuances of truth.

Consider dishonesty as a continuum, with total fabrications on one extreme and the tiniest of white lies on the other end.

SOME POINTS ALONG THE WAY WOULD INCLUDE:

- *Little fibs*

- *Exaggerations*

- *Deceptions*

- *Disingenuous arguments*

- *Inaccurate facts*

- *Plagiarism*

- *The big lie*

Each of these transgressions are easy traps to fall into and are far too common in many people's professional and personal communications. Little fibs, exaggerations, and deceptions can be easily rationalized as only minor ethical breakdowns in the pursuit of a pressing objective. But in time they will still cause trouble for their perpetrator.

Disingenuity is hapless and unnecessary. Why win an argument on a bogus premise? In such instances, winning is really losing.

Plagiarism is also far too common. You will note that I have peppered this book with numerous quotes, all of which have been attributed to their source. Far be it for me to denigrate the Beatles, Humphrey Bogart, or Stephen R. Covey, among others, by failing to attribute their work.

A professional friend, Dr. Linda Clever, often paraphrased Mark Twain, who said, "Always tell the truth, it is easier to remember." So true, Linda.

MINI STEPS TO SUCCESS

1. Resolve to never, ever, write or say something that is not true.

2. Review everything that you write in order to determine if anything you have written fails the truth test. Likewise, examine your prepared remarks in advance to confirm that they contain nothing that is untrue.

3. When you do slip and say something that is not true, admit your transgression quickly, clarify the record, and move on.

4. Examine the writings or remarks of others. If something appears false or disingenuous, follow up with them.

———THE TAKEAWAY———

Recognize that dishonesty falls along a broad continuum of communication, from outright fabrication to seemingly disingenuous deception. Avoid mistruths of any kind. At the end of the day, they will come back to haunt you.

Of all of our inventions for mass communication, pictures still speak the most universally understood language.
—animation pioneer Walt Disney

77

KABOOM!
MASS COMMUNICATION
THROUGH VISUAL SOCIAL MEDIA

AS OF THIS WRITING, my wife and I have been married 40 years and our only child, Ryan, is now 34. Between 2000 and 2018, Ryan battled drug addiction and endured a cumulative eight years of incarceration for nonviolent drug offenses. During his struggles, we learned that addiction is a disease and that our son's struggle to overcome it was largely beyond our control. And we never for a minute lost faith in him.

Ryan was released from prison in March 2019. Since then, he has maintained his sobriety and spends a good part of every day caring for his toddler son and loving partner. He also established a YouTube channel in late 2019 as a vehicle to tell his story and give the public a fuller understanding of addiction as well as the horrors of incarceration. Ryan quickly grew his channel subscriber base to about 12,000 subscribers. Recently, he invited me to do my own 10-week YouTube series from a parent's perspective, which he labeled "Frank's Friday."

My Frank's Friday experience has been a game changer. So far, each episode has been seen by more than 8,000 viewers who provide copious feedback through their comments. Prior to my YouTube posts, I had hoped to share my views on addiction and the failings of the criminal justice system by speaking to local community groups. It never came to pass. Yet here I was speaking to people all over the world each week. I am overwhelmed by the potential of this platform.

A book about communication would be lacking if I did not address the concept of mass communication through *visual* social media, which I believe is the wave of the future. If I can engage with thousands of people every week to tell my story, then I assure you, anyone can.

At a minimum, recognize the enormous power of the YouTube platform. The preceding 76 chapters of this book are intended to help readers communicate more effectively in one-on-one encounters, small groups, and large public arenas. Embracing visual social media can help you communicate with the world.

MINI STEPS TO SUCCESS

1. As people read less, they will eyeball more. The future of communication appears inexorably wed to visual media such as video.

2. Get experience shooting, editing, and distributing video. At first you may opt to produce simple videos on a mobile device that can in turn be distributed on Facebook or through other platforms. Such a toe-in-the-water experience is likely to be invaluable for you down the road.

3. As you learn social media video production, recognize that the effectiveness of your video

presence goes well beyond sharing useful information in talking-head mode. Integrate other visual effects; use multiple modalities and manage background and lighting for optimal effect.

———THE TAKEAWAY———

Rapid advances in visual social media are making it easy to communicate with large groups of people throughout the world from the comfort of your home. Understand the extraordinary power of the medium. Better yet, share your passion with others through YouTube and other video-oriented social media platforms.

EPILOGUE

Ever since the first intelligent beings inhabited our planet, communication has been central to existence. Every creature, from humans on down, communicates with others, either verbally or through some other mutually understood mechanism. Life could not go on without effective communication.

Effective communication encompasses a vast swath of subject matter, too broad for any mortal to cover adequately in its entirety. But the process of writing this book has been fun and educational for me as I have tried to make an impact on would-be effective communicators.

I have consciously tried to make things clear and simple. Hopefully you, the reader, can take something from the book that will help you minimize misunderstandings with others and enrich your personal life and professional career.

Beyond our DNA, we invariably seem to be products of our parents and their values. My parents lived long, happy lives, but each has been deceased more than 25 years. Only after their deaths did I recognize that I inherited one touching and invaluable trait from each of them.

My mother was an optimist, a happy warrior. As the saying goes, "she never met a stranger." Even in supermarket lines she would invariably break into conversation with anyone and everyone. When I was young, whenever I was down, my mother would hug me and say, "Don't worry; everything will be okay." And, of course, she was always right.

My father, for his part, was kind, loving, and always sided with the underdog. A proud, extroverted, handsome man, he perpetually found time for those less fortunate. He befriended numerous lost souls whom society considered outcasts. As a young child, I frequently watched sports events on television. Often my father would enter the room and ask, "Who's the underdog." Sure enough, he cheered his heart out for that team.

It turns out that I became a composite of my parents. Several lifelong friends have told me that I am the most optimistic person they have ever met, and I have continually cast my lot with the less fortunate. I have tried to pass this philosophy on to our son as I repeatedly tell him that my primary wish is for him to have a happy life and commit to being of service to others.

I share the same wish for all my friends, old and new, who have been kind enough to read this book. Enjoy life every hour of every day, for we all go around only once, and try to be there for others. Becoming a more effective communicator is a perfect way to start.

ACKNOWLEDGMENTS

I am grateful to Joan Tapper and Isabelle Walker for their exceptional and professional work as editors for this book and to John Balkwill for his management of the layout process. Thanks, as well, to my professional partner, Mitch Goddard, and to my wife, Diane, who graciously allowed me to disappear into my home office for hours at a time.

COMPANY OVERVIEW

The 77 Group is a privately held company established by Mitch Goddard and Frank Leone (see About the Author) in 2020. The company's goal is to work with individuals and business entities in order to enhance their communication and leadership capabilities through books, YouTube-based training, and personalized internet training, among other means.

> *The 77 Group's Mission Statement:*
> *To utilize the principals' 100-plus years of senior professional and military-based experience in order to provide immediately applicable communication and leadership skills to both individuals and organizational personnel in order to substantially affect their ability to interact with others on both a professional and personnel level.*

About Mitch Goddard

Mitch Goddard, CPC, ELI-MP, is co-founder of The 77 Group. Mr. Goddard is President and CEO of Vivian-Grace Associates, a consulting group specializing in executive performance and workforce engagement and Executive Director of The Goddard Leadership Institute, which he founded in 2017.

Mr. Goddard has served in executive leadership roles across a spectrum of industries including hospitality and health care and multiple roles with the Department of Defense.

He has focused on effectively assembling and leading high-performing teams with wide-ranging skills while adapting to diverse and changing missions and environments. He has also served as keynote speaker for professional groups and organizations.

Mr. Goddard studied business and organizational development at the University of Southern California (USC), California State University Northridge, and Eastern Oregon State University. He and his wife, Carolann, live in Hanford, California. They are active in their church and enjoy travel and gardening.

About the partnership he says, "I am pleased and inspired to partner with my dear friend Frank Leone. I believe our shared values, diverse backgrounds, and decades of combined real-life experience uniquely position us to offer practical, easy to apply, insight to support the personal and professional growth of others."

ABOUT THE AUTHOR

Frank H. Leone, MBA, MPH, is co-founder of The 77 Group. Mr. Leone served as President and CEO of RYAN Associates and founder and Executive Director of the 2,200-member National Association of Occupational Health Professionals (NAOHP) for 31 years before selling both entities in 2016.

Mr. Leone has spoken before hundreds of groups, large and small, provided numerous training sessions in communication, and maintains a deep interest in public speaking and all aspects of communication. Prior to establishing RYAN Associates in 1985, he served as a social scientist for the RAND Corporation and as a hospital administrator at the University of Massachusetts Medical Center.

Mr. Leone is a graduate of Vanderbilt University and holds an MBA in Marketing from the Olin Graduate School of Management at Babson College, and an MPH in Health Administration/Health Education from the Fielding School of Public Health at UCLA. He lives with his wife, Diane, and Labrador retriever, Brava, in Santa Barbara, California.

About the 77 Group partnership, he says, "I am extremely excited about engaging in a joint effort with Mitch. On one hand, we have incredible respect for one another, yet on another level we possess a distinctly different skill set. Mitch is 'Mr. Leadership,' whereas I am confident about my communication expertise."